wild on her blue days

wild on her blue days

Edited by
Lynn Michell & Helen Boden

AmberSandPress

Published in the UK by
AmberSandPress
6B Mortonhall Road
EDINBURGH
EH9 2HW
info@AmberSand.co.uk

The publisher acknowledges the financial support of a grant from the
Scottish Arts Council under the Awards for All programme

ISBN 0-9550488-1-8

Typeset and designed by Initial Typesetting Services, Edinburgh
Printed and bound by MPG Books Ltd, Bodmin

Contents

place

sense

challenge

re/solution

Acknowledgements

The editors are grateful for a grant from the Scottish Arts Council under the Awards for All scheme towards the production of this anthology.

We sincerely thank Ian Heslop and Val Duncan of the Salisbury Centre, and Keith Smith from the Southside Community Centre, Edinburgh, for believing in this project and for providing support and encouragement from the beginning.

We are grateful to Fiona Stewart for taking on the administrative work and for her quiet wisdom.

Thanks also to Claudine Meyer for her skills in chairing the AmberSand committee meetings and for her commitment and enthusiasm, and to Judith Fox and Alison Wheelwright for proof-reading. Many thanks too to Carolann Martin (ITS) for type-setting the manuscript.

We are delighted with the original artwork which Cara Forbes and Nye Stenning have produced.

Heartfelt thanks and apologies to Nye Stenning who had to dismantle and re-build Lynn's computer several times during the final weeks of this project.

Of course our gratitude goes to the many friends and colleagues who have given us advice and assistance, including Sarah Austen, Larry Butler, Fiona Farris, Matthew Gibson, Mike Hall, Elaine Henry, Jim Hughes, Fran Lavandel, Rowena Love, James McKinna, Gill Plain, Gary Smith, Justine Stansfield and Stephanie Taylor.

Most of all we want to say a huge thank you to the writers who inspired us to put together this anthology.

Inroduction: The Writing Room

Come, let me write. And to what end? To ease
A burdened heart.
(Sir Philip Sidney)

The class provides an environment in which we can tap into our creativity … and
we write. In writing we express our deepest emotions, sometimes capturing feelings
we did not know were there. Putting them on paper, making them conscious, more
transparent, clearer, may help us to deal with these feelings and move on. So the
next time we write, the emotion we express may have moved on too. And so the cycle
continues.
(Judy Bury, writer from Salisbury Centre writing group)

Helen and Lynn:

This anthology came into being because writing produced by talented
individuals who have worked with us grew into a collection of prose and
verse that we felt deserved a wider audience. *Wild on her Blue Days* showcases
their achievement.

We established Writing Room to provide classes in creative and therapeutic writing and other literary activities. It has no single, fixed physical
location, but happens wherever we set with up the intention of producing
and sharing writing, sometimes even outdoors. However, we do have some
favourite venues, or spiritual homes, in the Edinburgh area, where we have
established regular, long-running classes. These include the Salisbury
Centre, the holistic education centre on the Southern fringes of the city,
close by Arthur's Seat; and the Southside Community Centre, a converted
church on the busy thoroughfare to and from the city centre. We have also
run classes and facilitated courses at the Theosophical Society in the New

Town, and the Ca(i)re Project in Morningside as well as a number of one-off workshops in a variety of settings in Edinburgh and beyond, for example at book fairs and arts festivals, or as tie-in projects with art exhibitions. Sometimes we run courses or workshops for specific groups, such as carers, or people with mental health problems. Sometimes we offer a day, or a series of evenings, devoted to writing on a specific topic or theme. These have included: colour, metaphor, the elements, change and transition, the body, food, and life journeys. Some writers choose to work in a one-to-one setting with one of us. Participants from all these contexts have contributed work to this anthology.

We work as two individuals in collaboration. Like all our clients and participants, we have different styles and creative approaches. Below, and in the introductions to each of the five sections, we each describe our particular take on what Writing Room is about, and how *Wild on her Blue Days* has come together.

Helen:

We believe that anyone with basic literacy skills can enjoy and benefit from creative writing, but that many of us need to be given permission to do so. So many aspects of life today encourage a damaging separation of body, mind and spirit, that it can be difficult to have the conviction to live creatively or to make time for creative activity. The dedicated space and supportive atmosphere of the Writing Room is often hugely important for inexperienced or unconfident writers in this respect. We aim to allow participants to find their own voice. This takes two complementary routes: by closely examining and validating personal experience; and through enjoyable exercises designed to access creativity and evade the 'inner critic', that negative voice that makes us edit and censor our material before it even gets onto the page. We work both by responding intuitively and organically to the situations participants present, and by engaging them in task-oriented, structured processes. Both approaches help to elicit an authentic personal response that avoids cliché and bypasses the beginner's perceptions about what poetry, or a short story, 'should' be about, contain or sound like.

The idea is to help provide the best conditions for creativity. We regard writing not just as a cerebral activity but as a physical, embodied process and an emotional and spiritual experience. Typically, we might first turn inward, in a relaxation or visualisation exercise, so that each participant can re-connect with him/herself. Then they can begin to discover what they need from the session, and to access a sense of stillness, clarity and ease that unleashes a flow of creative possibility. Or we might start with a group warm-up or word-game. Sessions can take a multi-artform approach, sometimes, where viable, incorporating movement, music or visual art. Each form prepares the way for the next — within each session, or throughout a longer course. All these approaches also help to free the writer from anxiety about what to put on the blank piece of paper in front of them. The techniques known as 'automatic writing' or 'flow-writing' were the starting-point for a lot of pieces included here. This involves 'splurging' onto the paper what needs to be said in a rapid, uncensored way. Sometimes this produces an amazing stream of consciousness which requires little or no further work; sometimes it is more of a brainstorming exercise to provide the writer with a resource they can go on to develop into polished verse or prose — within the session or later, on their own. *Wild on her Blue Days* contains both spontaneous pieces written quickly in class, and more crafted work that has undergone considerable revision.

We are committed to the idea of writing for wellbeing and sustenance. At the very least we hope that writers will experience an increased sense of enjoyment and achievement. Some of our work goes further than this and has a clear 'therapeutic' slant, although we are writers, not therapists, and do not consider what we do to be a substitute for therapy or medical treatment. But in conjunction with them, creative writing is inherently therapeutic, and as such can be hugely beneficial for those suffering from a wide range of physical and mental illnesses. As a tool for exploring health issues and problems, it leads directly to reduced stress and increased understanding and empowerment. It also works indirectly, by providing a diversion in the form of a meaningful and stimulating activity. At its most basic, but perhaps most important level, language, especially poetry, is therapeutic because its rhythms and sounds themselves have soothing, healing qualities. Creative writing enables those undergoing medical treatments to rediscover their sense of identity as individuals, and to communicate things they may find difficult or impossible to express in speech. And it can also facilitate speech, when writings are shared and become readings. The process of reading one's work furthers the therapeutic process, by establishing connections with others. Each participant works at their own level and pace within a supportive group. Confidentiality within the therapeutic group setting is always maintained and privacy respected:

reading and sharing experiences are optional. Writing is viewed both as a means to an end – a tool for exploring issues and developing self-confidence, motivation and articulacy – and an end in itself. Process and product are seen as being of equal importance, although the relative emphasis placed on each can vary considerably between groups, and between different sessions with the same group.

A lot of the work included here had its origins in 'therapeutic writing' groups. The holistic, incremental approaches used in these settings and with beginners have also helped more experienced writers to generate fresh ideas, work through blocks, or structure larger writing projects. Some groups, especially those which have been running for some time, come to focus on the development of writing skills, including editing and polishing, often of work developed outwith the class. Some of these 'writing critique' classes continue also to emphasise the value of writing within the group setting, in the presence of other members; where appropriate we too participate in the writing exercises.

We live in a fast-paced, consumer-oriented society, where there is insufficient political will to celebrate, much less promote, creativity. This means that our work, especially that at the 'therapeutic' end of the scale, runs the risk of being dismissed as self-indulgent and irrelevant. But this approach comes from a long tradition, of which scant few of today's leaders are aware. The first quotation in the epigraph, for example, is from Sir Philip Sidney's sonnet sequence *Astrophil and Stella*, written in 1581–82, and published in 1591. Sidney presents an imaginary dialogue with an opponent who taunts him that he should be ashamed of publicising his distress, and will be thought foolish. Despite – or because of – this he retains his conviction that therapeutic writing is the way to exorcise his demons: 'What harder thing to smart and not to speak?' In keeping with the fashion of the time, the speaker's sentiment is knowing and partly self-deprecating, and crafted into a stylised and tightly-disciplined form. So far we haven't set a sonnet-writing exercise, though we could and some day might, but we have covered other literary forms, such as haiku, or, indeed, using dialogue to explore the experience of 'being in two minds' about something. Such disciplines help to demonstrate how the apparent constraints of a literary structure can paradoxically be liberating — as well as providing no small sense of satis-faction at having transformed one's initially 'formless' personal experience into an artifact that has the power to communicate to others. And of course we do not confine ourselves to venerable old forms. Sonneteering would have come naturally to writers in the sixteenth century; in the twenty-first, the multiculturally-influenced rhythms of rap and urban music are more likely to inform our writing. It may not be a co-incidence that a number of our clients write spontaneously in verse.

Unsurprisingly in a city like Edinburgh, many of our venues have a history of use for literary purposes: the Writing Rooms themselves are part of a long creative tradition. The present Salisbury Centre was between 1806 and 1830 the family home of William Blackwood, founder of *Blackwood's Edinburgh Magazine,* whose contributors included James Hogg, the 'Ettrick Shepherd', author of *Confessions of a Justified Sinner;* and Thomas De Quincey, 'The English Opium Eater'. Joseph Conrad's *Heart of Darkness,* arguably the first twentieth century novel, was commissioned by *Blackwood's.* Writers promoted by Blackwood were by no means exclusively male. In 1818 he published a novel called *Marriage* by Susan Ferrier, an Edinburgh writer with greater sensitivity to issues of national identity than her more famous contemporary Jane Austen. Early visitors to the house that became the Salisbury Centre included James Hogg, De Quincey and Sir Walter Scott.

On the other side of the city, in the New Town, is the Edinburgh branch of the Theosophical Society, the organisation founded by Madame Blavatsky in 1875. Theosophy emphasises the interrelatedness of all forms of life. It encourages the study of comparative religion, philosophy and science, and the investigation of unexplained natural phenomena and human powers. The Theosophical Society's large first-floor drawing room and library now doubles as a studio space for activities including tai chi, Alexander Technique, meditation – and holistic, multi-artform writing groups.

Lynn:

I started my first creative writing group in the Salisbury Centre three years ago and groups have met once or twice a week there ever since. There are other places where I facilitate both workshops and weekly classes, but I think of the Salisbury Centre as the place where I have my roots as a writing teacher. We work in the beautiful, south-facing library which often seems alive with its own spirit, perhaps because writers, editors and publishers have used this room in the past and have left behind something of themselves. On the door is a notice which says 'no food, no drinks, no cats'. But we are free creative spirits and so we let in Deva the cat, we drink tea and sip water, and sometimes when we are celebrating we bring food to share. We break the rules, just as I encourage writers to break internalised rules about writing. I tell them to find their own voices and to ignore preconceptions about what is or is not allowed. I want to set them free to express themselves truthfully and clearly.

So what takes place when I quietly close the door to begin a session and look at the expectant faces around the table? In that room I create a safe, nurturing space in which people feel free to say and write whatever they want, knowing that they will not be judged or criticised. The women (and my groups have been almost exclusively women) create strong bonds with one another as they recognise and acknowledge what others relate. Individual experience is validated and multiplied. The process of writing brings into focus a sense of self as layers of experience are peeled back, exposing what lies beneath. It takes us into surprising places and spaces where we find the clues and solutions to the way we feel and the way we experience the world. Writing is a tool and a catalyst; it is a process and an end product. It clarifies, reveals and explains. We write, we are taken by surprise as words tumble on to the page, we understand ourselves better for what we have written, and so we grow and change and move on.

At the start of every session, I ask the people round the table to hold hands to form a circle. We close our eyes and spend a few minutes calming the breath and relaxing our bodies. I invite everyone to leave behind the events which happened before the class. I ask them to concentrate on the touch of hands, the joining of the circle, the feelings of trust around the table. Even after five minutes of quiet breathing, it is difficult to let go of one another's hands, but now we are quietened and open to what will happen next.

Aware that I am often treading on egg-shells and shifting sands, I work very intuitively, and while I plan in outline a session or series of sessions, I may well abandon my ideas as I enter the room and sense the mood and the needs of the writers around the table on any particular day. With one women-only group, I focused on the four elements as a way of showing members how they can bring to any topic or theme what they personally want to explore. When I invite them to meditate on falling rain, or to visualise surf and sea, they know they can go their own way – and they do. They quickly learn that I do not prescribe or expect. If one day I play gentle music and suggest the peace and harmony of an empty room or landscape, they are completely free to turn their backs on my suggestions and follow their own thoughts. One week I brought in a blue glass bowl, filled it with water and floated white flowers on the surface. The women talked about the healing properties of water, but one who had remained silent said, 'I can't relate to any of this. For me, water is difficult. I have to push myself through a barrier of fear even to get into the shower.' Her writing took her response further as she related how she had been frightened of getting into a swimming pool as a child. And so people set off on their own journeys, finding within a wide and general starting point what is meaningful to them as individuals.

One day I had planned a session on the gentle, healing power of warmth, wanting to steer clear of the more terrifying and destructive properties of fire since there are some fragile women in the group who cope valiantly and bravely with difficult problems. During the previous four weeks we had written about air and wind, water and sea, and the mood of the group had remained sober, thoughtful and attentive as individuals recalled and wrote about past pain and loss. Time for a positive session, I thought. One of the women produced a wonderful stone burner which we lit and placed in the centre of the table. As we held our hands to the flame, we talked about occasions when we had been calmed and warmed by a fire. We recalled bonfires and open hearths and cooking. I played a Chopin Prelude and asked the women to visualise warmth finding a way into their bodies. Then the women wrote while I wondered how they would express their feelings of harmony. But as usual I was taken by surprise. One woman expressed her inability to imagine any healing; she wrote that she wished fire could burn her flesh, leaving her spirit pure and free. Another woman told the others for the first time that she suffered from manic-depression and that she spent her life waiting for the next unpredictable mood change. A third woman wept because her mother was ill and about to undergo surgery. All wrote about fire as transformation – a wish, a hope, an impossibility. And so my quiet session evolved into a powerful and moving one in which women wrote about raw, painful feelings and offered up their experiences for others to share. At the close there were many tears, but also a gentle coming together and a sense of moving on, of resolution. It felt like breathing out after holding a breath for too long.

I don't want to give the impression that all my classes and workshops are heavily cathartic, although inevitably some are. I remember one day in summer when we all danced in the garden of the Salisbury Centre with flowers in our hair. I remember us trying on wonderful, ridiculous hats and scarves and then role-playing the new women whose mantles we had taken on. There has been a short drama written for people sitting on a park bench, stories about doors and keys, poems about the crazy shapes we imagine our lives take, imaginary gifts in boxes, and a touchy-feely bag containing velvet, fake-fur and tissue paper.

Because I am also a glass artist, I often use the tools of my trade to inspire writing. Stained glass is unashamedly beautiful, especially the textured and painted pieces. I place these in the window to show up their rainbow colours before inviting people to chose the pieces which appeal to them or which match the theme we are working on. Always there are surprises, such as the writer who chose a small piece of amber and a piece of turquoise because long ago she lost a precious ear-ring while leaning over the railing of a ferry. Or the woman who chose red because it was the colour of her scars.

I can list topics I have covered, but I cannot really give you a full sense of the creative energy which flows in the room. Writers say so often, 'this is the only place where I can say this,' and 'I wouldn't say this to anyone else, but I feel I can here.' For all of them, trust and confidentiality is paramount. For a couple of hours, they are free to speak and write without anyone telling them they are being silly or exaggerating or getting upset about nothing. Here they find others who feel as they do. And we experience surprising synchronicity. I remember when we were working on characters, one woman read her piece about a mis-fit of a heroine who loved collecting buttons. Then the next women read a piece about the holocaust in which she described a woman whose 'job in the camp had been to remove and sort the buttons from the confiscated clothing of the new arrivals and from the discarded clothing of the victims herded to the gas chambers.'

I often witness a development in writing ability and in self-confidence among the writers who come to me. I have responded to this by setting up a gradation of classes. Initially some of those who come to the classes at the Salisbury Centre do so because their lives have thrown up questions and difficulties, and they want to sort out their thoughts and feelings by writing about them. Others may not have specific issues to deal with but have been writing journals and diaries for some time in solitude and are ready to take the big step of sharing what they have to say with others, as well as wanting to experiment with different forms and formats such as narrative, dialogue and poetry. The class is a place where they can play with words, shape, and form until they feel confident that they have found the voice which feels truly their own. Others are at a transitional point, perhaps because of illness or bereavement, a divorce or retirement. These women work hard at the issues they need to write about until there comes a moment when they know that there is no more to say. Having spilled out their hearts and written every which way about something which has been bottled up for a long time, they arrive at a point of equilibrium. Those who have explored personal issues in depth need, at some point, to move on. They are becoming interested in language, in the structure of written prose and poetry, and the ways in which they can translate personal experience into something which reaches out to a wider audience.

For these writers I run a different kind of class. In the 'grown-up class', as one writer has dubbed it, there is no holding hands, no music or movement, and no gradual release into writing. These sessions feel more like creative writing seminars in which people tackle all kinds of challenges, some of which they love and some of which they hate. But they are ready for these challenges. I still suggest a theme or idea at the start of each block of classes, but this starting point is very open and individuals are encouraged to do with it what they want. One term we started by considering the meaning of the phrase 'an act of violence'. Out of this came all kinds of stories and poems, no two alike in any way. I started another block of classes by putting on the table a pile of empty picture frames which prompted memories and ideas for stories. Sometimes we work on something specific, such as character development or a plot structure involving different time frames. Sometimes we experiment with different voices and forms. Sometimes, when everyone is absorbed in a writing project, I do nothing. In this class, the rule is that we offer constructive criticism. I want people to go away feeling that they have made a small (or big) step forwards. Like the more therapeutic classes, a strong bond has formed between members of this class, and although individuals come from different backgrounds, they feel able to say what they feel and think without fear of judgement or negative reprisal.

So far I have written about what I try to give to the writers. I must not omit what they give to me. There is the pleasure of watching individuals change, grow and develop, not just in their writing competence but in themselves. People arrive shy, hesitant and insecure and several weeks later when they find that what they write is eagerly received, they blossom into more confident, articulate and grounded human beings. They become more whole. There is the warm unity of a group of women who genuinely care for one another as they listen and read and share; it is a pleasure for me to be one link in this trusting circle. Finally, there is the sheer delight of the astonishing, surprising writing which people produce. I am frequently bowled over as I listen to poems and stories which are so powerful that they produce goose-bumps, tears and laughter. These are the gifts which I take away with me and which sustain me.

Helen and Lynn:

We view this anthology as an extension of our commitment to finding as many ways as possible of sharing writing. It has been compiled using a collaborative editorial process, with many contributors participating in the preparation of their work for publication — either on a one-to-one basis, or within the context of their class. Other pieces were produced during short writing exercises – sometimes as short as five minutes – within a class or workshop. We unashamedly include these alongside more polished work to demonstrate how setting aside even a small amount of time for writing can produce interesting and valuable results.

The contributors include established writers, those with no previous experience of creative writing, and all stages in between. They are aged from their early twenties to their nineties and come from many different backgrounds. A large percentage are women. Some have mental or physical health problems or learning difficulties. There are writers from America, Australia and Ireland, and writers of French, German, Malaysian and Swedish origin, writing in their second language.

Many of the pieces speak for themselves. To some, however, we have added a note or commentary to describe how the writing came into being. In a few cases, the author has written his or her own preface. There are five sections: lifestory, place, sense, challenge and re/solution. It was quite a challenge in itself to categorise some of the work submitted, and there is considerable thematic cross-over between sections: for example, some 'lifestory' or 'place' pieces were initially inspired by the right-brain techniques that stimulated much of the work for the 'sense' or 're/solution' sections. And work that seemed naturally to belong in 'place', such as site-specific exercises based in the immediate environment, took flight into fictive spaces far removed from its origins, and ended up in 're/solution'. In the end the categorisation was often quite arbitrary, and we hope the reader will dip in and out of the different sections and enjoy making his/her own links and connections.

Preface

The Salisbury Centre

Marjorie Wilson

You open the door and leave the world outside.

I can do without the troubles I take in with me – the strife, the strain and the worry. Why is there so much of it? Sometimes I think it can only stop when death steps in. But death has decided to hesitate, to stumble on the doorstep.

Not yet, it says.

Not yet.

lifestory

introductions

birth

childhood

growing

ageing

identity

transitions

generations

dying

lifestory

Helen:

We usually start work with a new group with an autobiographical approach: written selfportraits and snapshots of the present self, leading to lifestories and memories from the past. Beginning with the self, in the present, allows participants to sense who, and how, they are at the moment of writing, at the moment of embarking on a new experience, as well as how to introduce themselves to other members of the group. The request to revisit one's past is sometimes met with resistance, perhaps in the form of a participant's actual inability to remember several years from their childhood. These memories become clearer with the practice of inviting them in. For older writers there is pleasure in recording memories, often with younger relatives as the intended audience. For others, revisiting their pasts is a therapeutic, healing experience — or a source of material for fiction. Painful rites of passage, conflicts and losses can begin to be seen in a new light when written down and heard by an empathetic audience. And the lifestory can continue beyond the present: several writers here imagine what their later life, and death, could be like.

Lynn:

I use various devices (to borrow a term from one of my writers) to encourage the re-visiting of the past. I invite writers to bring in old toys and treasures which they have kept from childhood, or photographs from long ago, or we may play a childhood game like hop-scotch or cat's cradle. Sometimes I play gentle lullaby music and ask each person to shrink back, like Alice, to a younger, smaller self. Was there one episode in their childhood which was pivotal in that it changed them irreversibly? Was there a period of pain or intense happiness? Sometimes it is easier to approach these sharp or poignant times through a medium other than writing, perhaps using coloured pens and paper; it is a bit like looking at something out of the corner of your eye rather than gazing at it full on. I ask writers to draw the shape or trajectory of their lives using crayons, or to make a collage. The results always amaze me: the edge of a long beach snaking round the paper, the meeting of sand and sea marked either by pink or black hearts to signify pleasure and pain; metal cages interlocked in an elaborate geometric shape with a female figure trying to manoeuvre her way through them as she copes with life's multiple demands. Translating shape and colour into writing is less threatening than simply starting with a blank sheet of paper, and can be much more revealing.

I Am

M R McDonald

I am at one with life in myself
I am the intellect of my own 'being in thought'
I am the source of my own poetic imagination
I am the voice of my own inspired thought
I am the depth of my being's innermost self
I AM – no matter who knows it.

Blue Velvet Dress

Fiona Stewart

I am 9, standing high,
the wind blowing about me,
in my mother's blue velvet dress.
I am shrunk, pulled back into the womb.
Now she is wearing the dress,
part of it inside with me,
enveloped in her sadness.

As a bird, I leave the nest,
still cloaked in blue velvet.
Flying through peaceful skies,
I remain shrouded in this gown.
The storms of life come along.
It tears.

Scraps of velvet fall from my body,
more and more until almost nothing is left,
except a growing sense of freedom within.

Shoes

Marjorie Wilson

How long had I been wearing the shoes? The black patent and white kid shoes? I must have started wearing them when they were large, loose and comfortable, but they gradually got smaller and tighter and more un-comfortable but I couldn't bear to stop wearing them. Life without my black patent and white kid shoes? Impossible. Unimaginable! I would go on bearing the discomfort and the pain. The patent was scuffed. The white kid was not white any longer – grubby, soiled and disreputable. The blisters were painful, especially on my heels. Say nothing. Not done to complain. Could I split them at the heels and then nobody would know? I started to limp. My face was twisted with suffering. I loved them so much. I would not be parted from them. Like my black satin bonnet with the rosebud at one side and the satin ribbon tied in a bow under my chin.

But one day the shoes disappeared. They were gone! Out of my life – my black patent and white kid shoes!

But they still exist in my memory and of course the photographs.

We had brought in belongings and photographs from our childhoods and had reflected on our possessions and their meanings. Marjorie Wilson, now 93 years old, recalled these shoes worn and loved when she was very young.

A Special Street Party

Barbara Stone

Chubby young fingers edge round the special celebratory tablecloth. Arms and legs both fully stretched, toes pointed, pirouette style, yet still I am too small to see the full banquet of food above me. Different aromas come from each trestle table, but it is the sweet-smelling table that is attracting the children, like bees to a honey pot. Strong maternal arms gather round my waist, lifting me to ponder over my choice of sweets. I fill my plate with old favourites, chocolate soldiers, snowballs and fairy cakes laid out on a bed of nuts and liquorice allsorts. I sit down on the grass, despite wearing my best dress, and happily tuck into my feast, ingesting too the warm summer air alive with the chatter of friends and neighbours.

I am five. I know that it is a special day, the Queen's special day, her coronation day. Special food, and special activities. I love to run and chase the wind, and the high feeling of swift movement through the air of this special June day. My friends join me in the races, the obstacle, the three-legged and the sack races. Parents, brothers and sisters wave flags to cheer their family on. A magic day!

Day turns to night, and still the magic goes on. Coloured lights, hanging from trees, vie with Scottish dance music to seek and hold attention. This seems a strange adult world, but the grasp of my mother's hand in mine comforts my fears. I mimic the movements of fast flowing dances, beating my feet in rhythm. Alas, too tired, I slip and fall. I skin my knee. It's time to end this special day. And perhaps a scar on my knee, my personal momento, will connect this ending with some future special day.

Sibling

Ajak

Mummy brought a baby back and put it in MY cot I never said I wanted one and no-one asked me why I crawled beneath the couch and stayed there for a day I didn't tell them what was wrong they didn't pull me out they called it by a funny name and put it in MY pram I bit its little fingers hard and said it was the dog they sent the dog away for good and didn't tell me where they kept the baby in their room to cry and cry and cry I held my hand across its mouth but never shut it up it wriggled like a slimy slug then turned a pinkish red I never told another one I wished that it was dead.

Leaving

Paula Cowie

Leaving bed

    for the stairs   AGAIN

      soft pyjamas

        cuddly ted

          the solitary bottom step

big noises   drunken shrieks   broken glass

        AGAIN

Leaving the stairs

    the other side of the door

    a room full of silly adults

    a small presence

    a silent plea

    no-one notices

        AGAIN

    Leaving them to it.

    Back to bed.

We had been working on memories of childhood, using music and visualisation. Writers were asked to recall a time which had a profound effect on the rest of their lives.

Sitting Amongst the Peas

Elke Williams

Jump
    Jump
        Jump
            Down the steps

    Skip
Skip   Skip on the garden path,

Hmm, I'm hungry,
What can I have?

        Skip
Skip   Skip

What can   I   have ?

What can   I   have ?

Not the apples and strawberries
But the carrots and peas!
Nobody watch me
I'm looking for peas.

Carrots and peas
Carrots and peas

Here are the peas!
I'm right in there
The bushes are high
Nobody can see me!

Snap off some pods
How big and green!
Open them gently
Crunch and eat.

How delicious can delicious be!

A deliberately delicate, child-like poem, where form echoes content, from a writer who
more often reflects on the pain and complexity of eating (see 'Precious Food' p73).

My Friends, Mah Future!

Ajak

Where do you find them?
my mummy asks
who will employ them?
bee hive hairdos an mini skirts round fat bums
showin stocking tops, introducin tights.
Them's people, ah thought,
an stans back an questions mah choice.

Ah roll up mah school skirt it the waist
wear bobby socks in lime nicked oot ay Wooly's
ah stretch oot mah curls the height ay mah face
spray laquer on an
ah dae want a job an
who will employ them?
rings in mah ears.

Boyfriend

Ajak

So I'm grown up now with a boyfriend stepping out
Doing what the others do, following a pattern
Young love touching feeling reaching out to a wedding day
Big day, lots of planning
Plan a baby but only after the house furniture is right
To be right she cried all night
He got drunk
Love's withering away
Falling apart
Nothing is
Right out of control.

My Child

Susan Bowyer

Some days I think I'm almost ready for you. So many questions to ask, holding back the moment I may meet you. My fears, so many and so selfish.

I see myself, growing around you. Protecting and nourishing you. Another sea inside where you will float before you set sail for dry land.

I imagine you, confident and fearless beside me. The patterns changed in time, releasing the past.

This was one of those surprise pieces which came from the heart and was not related to the starting point given.

There Are Moments in a Life

Ann Vilen

There are moments in a life that make you dizzy, moments when, if you look down at your feet, you'll swear the Earth really is spinning.

When my friends, Jon and Ginny, moved last summer, I stood on my porch in North Carolina, staring at their fully loaded truck framed by a landscape of mountains and morning birds. Suddenly, the same way a squirrel once lept from the kerb and fatally lodged itself between the spokes of my bike wheel, Mr. Reid my 7th grade science teacher's voice went off in my head, telling me that the Earth spins at a constant rate of 700 miles per hour. He was dead before I turned 13. I remembered that too, and in the same instant wondered why he'd come back to me nearly thirty years later, as Ginny and Jon stood in my driveway plotting the most direct route north. When Ginny looked up, I had to bite my lip to hold back tears. Our galaxy is hurtling toward Virgo faster than a supersonic jet. The universe is continually and irrevocably expanding at an unimaginable speed. Still, all my memories of this friendship are preserved in a single quart jar of home-canned peaches, floating like slippery planets in a mist of sugar. I won't open this last jar, even though my mouth waters for the taste of summer, because I know it is the legacy of nine seasons of steaming jars and skinning fruit and sweating side by side over the canner in Ginny's kitchen. Nine seasons revolving around the birthdays of our first-born children, the hills and the valleys of our marriages, the traditions of autumn car pools, Solstice dinners, Easter camping, July peaches.

A month later, I'd moved too. Taken my husband, two kids, two cats, two cars, a household of furniture and flotsam to a new house in another city, and put all but the human beings into storage so that we could move yet again. This time without the furniture or the flotsam (or the cars and cats), overseas to another country, another culture, another life.

Most days still, I wake up to the noise of buses and my neighbor's building skulking close to mine and the stiff North Sea wind batting branches against the window, and I ask myself, how did I get here? I can feel the Earth's mantle flapping in the breeze, the edges of the continents wafting slightly, like flying carpets preparing for lift off. My life has been a series of departures, unresolved endings, burned bridges, wild leaps, letting go. And now, as suddenly as the ghost of Mr. Reid accosted my memory, I hunger to keep things: hair on the barber's floor, an already mailed photograph, a lost pair of sneakers, a broken watch, a jar of last year's peaches, still sticky, with a tiny star crack in the glass just below the metal seal on one side. I hadn't noticed that before.

Poison Ivy

C MacLaverty

When we were kids, you walked us to the woods
where we ran, happy like mongrels
and you sat, fatherly, on a tree stump
with your notebook and pipe.
You taught us the names of wild flowers:
narcissus, foxglove, forget-me-not.

'The ivy will kill these trees eventually,' you said.
So we pulled stiff strips of green, marbled bunting
from wide trunks in satisfied ceremony.

Today, you are taking me to Asda.
City driving makes you grouchy but I'm too ill to go alone.
We park in the disabled space
and you fetch me a trolley.
Down the aisles, I think you look strange,
out of context: an anoraked author,
alone in Ready Meals.

I feel as if I cannot breathe for sadness.
The physical is easy, compared to this.
I'd swap anything, if you could
rip this ivy from my chest,
unsnare it from my neck.

At the checkout, you place a tin
of Bob the Builder spaghetti in my trolley
and hand me a pound coin to pay for it.
You know. How easily you know.

The Picture Frame

Claudine Meyer

I have been in this window for a while now, several weeks perhaps, certainly since the summer. And no one has even looked at me. It is just as well Mrs Twopenny, the owner of the shop, has not noticed I am still here, otherwise I would have already been relegated to the 'bargain box' below the stairs. I don't want to be there; I have many years to go yet. I am hardly scratched at all; I was polished when I arrived.

I would like a home, a proper home that is. I would like to hold the photograph of someone beloved. I have done that all my life. It has been a good life but right now, in the shop window, I am no use to anyone and I am bored.

I am going to do my very best to attract someone's attention. The sun is shining, I am going to catch some rays and send a signal to someone passing by. That is it, I have done it. That woman with the short purplish hair, dark glasses and black coat saw me. She is moving on; what a shame. Surely, she has a use for me. I would make a good present. Hang on! She is coming back. She is inside the shop, asking about me. It worked. Please buy me! I am not that expensive! I can't hide the couple of scratches and that piece of blue paper behind the glass does nothing for me at all. But you'll see, once you cover the blue paper with a photo, I'll be alive!

She is taking me. In a jiffy I am in a piece of dirty bubble wrap, and an old supermarket bag and we are off! This is so exciting! Where are we going? What is she going to do with me? I think we are in a car now. I am not good at travelling. How long will it take? We are stopping now. She grabs the bag. I hear keys. She walks in, puts me down gently. That is a good sign. She takes me out. I can see her properly now. Nice home, feels warm and clean, roomy. Lots of pictures around, lots of photographs. She likes art. Please put me in a prominent position! In a few years I'll be an antique, you know. She seems to hesitate. Finally she places me on a flat brown shiny surface. Wood, I think. Lots of photographs around me. Competition, I fear!

I am no mean frame. I was a commission to a silversmith no less, in Paris, from a foreign woman, no less. She had met him at a dinner party and she wanted a special frame to hold her baby grand-daughter's photograph. A gift for her daughter. Even the photographer was a star in Paris. Jean Delarue, I recall. You must have heard of him, surely. The foreign woman's daughter loved me at first sight. No wonder! I was all new and shiny, and I had been wrapped up in some extremely smart paper. 'Oh, merci maman, c'est magnifique,' she exclaimed, kissing her mother on both cheeks. And she took me straight into her bedroom. It was 1923. It was the start of a very intimate relationship. I knew her well, and her family too. She was elegant and beautiful and she loved life. She loved her jewellery and her clothes. She loved beautiful things. And she loved me! First I was on the mantelpiece. But then we changed home, so I moved to her dressing table. We moved so many times I lost count. I do not even know where we were most of the time. I was so lucky; always packed first and very carefully even when she was in a hurry. I was special. She looked after me and I looked after the precious photograph. And I was always in her bedroom; she would always find a place for me. We spent fifty-five years together.

Twice when she brought a new picture I was excited but worried. Would she get rid of the first, the original, the one I was made for? Please please please keep it there. It's mine. I know your daughter is a woman now, but this photograph is mine!

She must have heard me. Do you know what she did? She placed my photo between two sheets of blue paper for protection. It was so clever. The new photo went on top. First her grand-daughter, big brown eyes, a full head of black hair, then much later, her grand-daughter's two children, bigger brown eyes, a little girl with a blue dress and a page boy haircut, and her brother in a brown suit. Children, more children, I love children!

And all that time I watched them all change, and grow, year after year.

I watched her grow older, still beautiful, still elegant, but older.

One day I don't quite know what happened. A stranger came in when she was out, and the next thing I knew I was in a dark plastic bag with a whole lot of other pieces of silver and some bronze statuettes. I felt us being rushed outside and thrown into some van. I heard the engine rev. We were later transferred to another van and went on a terribly long journey. I felt very sick all the way. I ended up on a stall in some kind of market in a place called London. The picture of the children was taken out. Miraculously the blue sheets clung to the first picture and it stayed with me. Someone bought me and kept me in a dark cupboard for a very long time; so long that I stopped counting the years. I was no use to anyone. I was tarnished. I wondered if I would ever see anyone again. Eventually the cupboard was opened, everything in it literally thrown into a box and taken to some place where people bid for lots. And our lot ended up here, in the antique shop in Edinburgh.

Once again I am back in a house. I don't know why but there is a familiar feel here. It's going to be my home, and it feels as if I belong. A bit like the places I was in at first, warm, with the smell of good cooking. The other frames are full of people. They seem friendly. I look more closely; I am anxious to know who they all are.

I can't believe it, I recognise them. I do, I swear I do. I can't believe this. It can't be true. I am shaking. I hope my new owner can't see it. I am going hot and cold. I wish I could cry. I wish I could tell her. These people in the other pictures, on the wall next to me, are the pictures of the old woman who bought me, of her daughter, her grand-daughter, her great grand-daughter with the big brown eyes, and her two children with even bigger brown eyes. And the picture I am going to hold proudly is of a little girl of around four who looks so much like these two. Unless I am mistaken this is six generations of a family, my family; in a different place, a foreign place, far away from Paris.

She turns me upside down; she opens my back. She is about to find my secret. She sees the first sheet of blue paper, lifts it gently, and there she finds the photograph that has been with me always. She is holding it, looking at it, and tears are pouring out of her eyes. She is transfixed, she can't move. She knows. She lays me face down, goes into another room, and comes back, holding a photograph of a baby, my baby, her mother, the same photograph as the one I have taken care of for all these eighty years.

Inspired by a tumble of empty picture frames on the table.

After Jenny Joseph

Debbie Hind

When I'm post menopausal
I shall wear what I like
I will learn to tap dance and twirl and sing a lot
and I shall skip down the high street wearing a feather boa and nothing else
and tell everyone how old I am.

I'll turn up for tea in fancy dress
sit down in a red and yellow juggler's outfit
and laugh at people's astonished faces.

And I will enter the age of 'sod it' with great aplomb
and throw my heart and soul into all the eccentricities
I've not allowed myself before.

They'll try and stop me of course
my family and friends will worry about the change
and ponder the reasons for my seemingly odd behaviour
could it be grief? should we stop her? maybe it's her age?

But I shall rise above the panic
and calmly state that now I am an old woman
I can cast aside all cumbersome unnecessaries
and concentrate on fun.

Blue

Marjorie Wilson

Life is full of nothingness.
What welcomes me when I go home?
A paw on my knee
Sitting alone in a beautiful sun-drenched garden
The Nellie Moser on the wall just
Bursting into beautiful flower
The creeper on the bower
Almost over now but bending
With the weight of its lovely blossom.
Self-pity.
What foolishness.
My life has been crammed with beauty and people to love.

Dead

Stephanie Taylor

I'm in the back of my mum's car. I am peering out through my head. My eyes feel strange, as though I can't physically move them, but I can see all around.

My mum looks upset. She's very pale and her jaw is rigid. I stare at the twitching sinews in her cheek. Jules sits beside her. They aren't talking.

It isn't raining but I wish for the sound of the window wipers to soothe me. Something isn't right.

I go to reach over and switch on the wipers but nothing happens. Nothing at all. I have not even moved a single muscle. I feel I have the will to move but my body will not obey. I am stuck in a body that will not function.

I start to panic.

It is a strange mental panic.

There is no raised heartbeat or adrenaline to back it up. Am I panicking at all? I start to wonder what is going on. I wish my mum and Jules would tell me. I wish I could ask them. I have tried to speak but can't even inhale, let alone force breath over my throat. Suddenly, I begin to pick up a thread of realisation about what's happening. Nobody is speaking but they are telling me. I can feel it coming off them; it's vibrating around and reaching me.

I am dead.

Dead.

They think I am dead.

They are taking me somewhere to bury me. Why aren't they taking me to the morgue? Where is my funeral? This doesn't make sense. Why would they just take me and bury me?

I don't feel dead.

I try to use all my energy and force to communicate with them. They still drive.

Is this what happens?

Your body dies then all you are left with is yourself?

Forever?

I can't stand it. I don't want to be alone feeling nothing for the rest of my life in the ground, watching the blackness.

I stay sitting for a while, which is of course all I can do. I thought there would be some sort of explanation, a revelation. My mum and Jules are sobbing. Their guilt and grief blankets them in layers. I can see it, thick and deep.
We are at the chosen spot now.
The hole has been dug.
For me.
This is it. I scream with all my might.
'I'm not dead. I'm NOT DEAD! See me! Hear me! I am NOT DEAD!'

It's too late. It has happened so quickly. I am in the hole. How have I died?
How can I face this loneliness forever?
I watch them staring down at me. They begin to drop the first bits of earth on me.
Something amazing happens.
I feel it! I feel it hitting my actual body. But with every hit the earth pierces my flesh and bits of my soul start escaping. I can see it! It's like wisps of spun sunlight. It is beautiful.

I am beautiful.

I am beautiful.

I am free…

When I Am Gone

Fiona Stewart

When they pack up my stuff in cardboard boxes, will they know how much each thing meant to me? I hope they wrap everything carefully in newspaper and use tissues for the most precious belongings. They won't know which things were treasured – objects gathered from trips abroad; jewellery worn only on special occasions. All full of memories, but only for me.

I wonder if they will take longer over my photos and letters, and tell my stories to others? My truth will then be laid bare, my privacy gone. When my poems are read, will they reveal the warmth I have kept hidden inside?

Will those who thought they knew me be surprised? Once my fragile heart is exposed, maybe I will be loved as I never have when alive, living afraid, not knowing how to share.

Remember

Elke Williams

Who will remember you when you have gone?
Does it matter that there is anyone
Who will remember
What you achieved and what you've done?

Is there anything you want to leave behind?
Will there merely be footprints in the sand
Or a momento
Showing that you tried to be loving, caring and kind?

But you were here on Mother Earth
Where there's a cycle
Of living and dying,
The assurance of death and of birth.
Will you give what's precious
To each friend
To treasure
Till their lives also end?

Or will you plant a tree in wilderness?
Or carve a sign in solid stone?
No one will see you
When you do it on your own.

Remember it is you who will have gone
And Mother Earth will stay.
Or will you, maybe,
Just be moving on?

October

Hazel MacPherson

Remember me when you are in a different place
And I, still here through passing years.
In my memory I see your hair, your eyes, your face.
No longer do we walk along the rocky shore
Sharing words, laughter, and singing rhymes.
There is silence in remembering,
Listening for a whisper or more
And thinking back to our together times.

If I should catch a glimpse of you
At the side of my vision, just meeting,
Or maybe in spectral form
Maybe too, in silent dreams,
Or, in morn's misty dawn,
Then memories would be real and solid
And all sad things would fly away
Away from the time that you left that space
In my morning, at the break of day.

Do you remember that still morning
When it was your time to leave
And I, left here in sorrow, would miss you like breath,
Like air, like rain?
I remember, as the stars went out
And the golden moon was no more,
And I felt that I would always feel
The same
The same
The same.

Quartet

Judith Fox

1. Disunity

My shoulders are a resonant gateway channeling the path of my spine, connecting the upper cerebral world with the lower physical world. If the gateway opens thought is translated to action. A one-way gate, my brain tells my body what to do, but the gate is resolute and fixed and my body cannot convey its convoluted and twisted message back to the source. A gate may be open or closed, one or the other, not both, and I am separated by the weight I carry and the need to support myself.

I am tired; tired of forming and constructing the bridges, struts and supports to link upper and lower, intellectual and visceral, cerebral and somatic.

I have no centre, no core. I transfer and transmit, construct and destruct the transient signals and traffic to filter the messages, to give them purpose and direction.

I am the gatekeeper, but I am not part of the journey.

I am fixed in time and space, you may act and move through me, but I have no will of my own.

I control and am controlled, fixed, and immutable. If I am receptive you flow through me; obstructive you force me in a way I will not go; resistant you force me.

Far better when impulses flow in resonant synchrony down neural pathways and synapses, opening and closing the gate of my being, soul to centre, fragile bridges spanning vast disjunctions, a choreography of immense proportions.

2. The View from Within

Granite, lead, gravity, a leviathan weight encased in concrete.
Constantly building the wall ahead of me, dragging the weight of my past behind me.

Eternity to wear away a single atom at a time.
Which weighs more – a pound of rock or a pound of feathers?

I am a fault line, at fault, split in two. One half wrapped around my soul, like a dead twin, a stone baby, always with me, fossilized emotion, petrified, the pearl forming around a single irritant seed. The other moving with a glacial weight and force strong enough to move boulders and wear mountains down to the sea, depositing me a long way from home.

Slow, inexorable progress. Objects once in motion continue.

Irresistible forces, immovable objects.

I need a frictionless surface to push this away from me, and a Michaelangelo to see inside the stone.

Blood red poppies bring opium sleep.

3. The Stirring

My strength is in my right hand, my left brain. There is wisdom deep down at the base of all things; at the root of my tale my bones tell my story.

My mother has her hands around my throat, but my anger is in my skin, my boundary, my contact with the outside world. But even that is ethereal and I constantly shed my skin, snakelike, transforming – what is inside must come out.

Where am I in this body?

In my throat and my mouth, behind the mask for the world, I am all the things I say and do not say, my shame and my guilt all on my tongue. I taste all the wrongs I have ever done.

I am not alone in this body heavy with the memories and core of forever. My stone twin lies under my heart, sleeping a fossilised dream, frozen before all of this happened. Sometimes I feel her move, restless in her deepness. Almost awakening but never being heard she whispers to me and tells me stories of the time when she was alive, before the dreaming.

4. The Whispering

'Who are you?'
'We are you, I am us.'

'Are you real?'
'Are you?'

'Where are you?'
'In the space between your heartbeats.'

She reaches a hand up to touch my heart from where she lies foetally curled beneath it.

'Am I real?'
'You sleep.'

'I don't understand.'
'We sleep.'

'Do we dream?'
'We dream each other. I was formed of the dreaming, solidified by need, a place for your dreams to wait their time.'

She flexes pink granite toes and snuggles down, turning away from me to sleep, returning to her embryonic dreams.

And now I understand.

My dreams have turned to stone but they have yet to be crushed to dust. My stone twin keeps them safe for me, close to my heart, frozen in their prenatal form. Protected against time, for the deep time when I pass through the circle again to enter the labyrinth.

One day she will be born. Until then we carry each other.

Writers were asked to draw and colour representations of their life journeys, using images to symbolise good times, painful times, crunch times and transitions. Judith Fox discovered through her artwork the leitmotifs which recurred along the way. Unlike most other pieces in this section, which offer a snapshot in time, 'Quartet' distils a lifetime into an abstract prose-poem.

place

rooms

interiors

exteriors

home

belonging

explorations

place

Helen:

My sessions on lifestory writing often conclude with an exercise that involves coming out of the 'role' of autobiographical subject. Focusing on the past regularly for long periods can become counterproductive as a creative and therapeutic technique if it is not balanced with attention to the present, to others, and to our environment; it seems important to maintain a dialogue between inner and outer. We take a variety of approaches to working with place. In the early weeks with a new group we'll shift attention from pure introspection, into the room, and onto the group experience, by introducing some site-specific and collaborative exercises. The room itself is important, but it is also incidental. It's great to work in places that are clearly conducive to creativity and healing, or to a particular kind of work or approach, such as movement, but any room where we set up with a group of people with the intention of producing and sharing writing becomes an appropriate Writing Room. Even if the physical environs don't look prepossessing, getting to know them is always fruitful, even if this means getting to know what we don't like, and why. A warmup can literally involve walking round the room, and sometimes beyond it, round the building. This is a way for new members to familiarise themselves with the environment, and for those who regard themselves as already familiar with it to notice something new, look at it in a fresh way, as though for the first time — to take in architectural or constructional features, decor, furniture, objects and ornaments. Writing that develops from this kind of stimulus often departs a long way from its site-specific origin, for example C Scott's 'The Book of the Dead', and some other pieces that appear in the final section, re/solution.

Once familiar with the local environment, we can go further: we visualise a trip out of the writing room, into places near and far, real and imaginary, from our past and present. Stories develop as locations start to interact with characters; poetry grows from the desire to capture the vocal register of these places.

Lynn:

When asked to imagine a place, real or imaginary, a writer can take the exercise at face value and concentrate on finding words to breath life into a room or a landscape: in the first piece the five rooms are characters in their own right that do not need to be peopled. More often, as soon as a figure is placed in the landscape, place is revealed as somewhere soaked in human emotion, in history and story. Place and person blend and bind together, as in Tom Britton's 'Rain-Swept Streets' and Ann Vilen's 'Crone Tree'. Place is more than place; it is image of and metaphor for human experience. A particular place may contain and hold a unique moment or memory and so become the keeper of a part of an individual's spirituality.

Rooms

Lisa Mayber

First: The Red Room

The room is large, wide, long. Not a very high ceiling, but high enough; white as the walls are white. A little shadowy in the corners at dusk. The floor and low skirting boards are of dark-stained wood. The far end of the room, away from the door, is entirely glass. White gauze curtains cover it.

The window faces north. All the light is cool. Outside, across a narrow stone terrace, is smooth close-cropped grass. One can walk down the gentle slope, across the valley and on to the hills beyond.

All there is in the room, covering almost all the floor, is a magnificant red Persian carpet, its complex patterns in shades of red, warm, bright, soft red.

Always the room is cool, quiet, and the red carpet glows richly.

Second: The Slip Room

The house has four bedrooms upstairs, two at the front facing the road and two at the back. The stairs and a long narrow cupboard, used for the ironing board, divide the back bedrooms, which look east onto the garden. The two bedrooms at the front are separated by a slip room barely six feet wide. In the sloping part of the ceiling is a skylight, high up so that one is not aware of the traffic outside. One sees only the sky.

Painted white, the room contains only a few cushions and, on the floor in the farthest corner, a plain lamp with a white glass globe shade. That stands to the right of the window, opposite the door.

The floor is covered with a velvet-soft grey carpet. Homespun cotton of a similar grey covers the cushions.

In the morning, facing west, the room is cool. When the sun is strong a white shade is drawn down over the window.

Third: The Library

Books line the walls of this old room. Most of them are old; their dark bindings make the room a little dim. The broad window faces north. Only a little sun reaches it at the beginning and end of the day. The pattern on the carpet is faded, unremarkable.

Diagonally across from the door, at right angles to the window, is a large old well-polished pedestal desk. A broad-seated upright chair is behind it. On the desk are writing implements in a brass tray and a brass lamp with a long horizontal shade. Next to it a standard lamp lights a high-backed comfortable chair.

Quietness is the charm of the room. Though part of a large house, and facing a road where buses and cars pass, it is secluded. And from the window the outlook is calm. A grey stone wall screens the road from the writer's view; it is high enough for only the tops of buses to be seen. Passers-by go unnoticed in the brief moment they cross the gateway.

Thick turf fills the square between the flagged pathway, the house and the stone wall. There are no flowers. Only a small tree grows close to the side wall, in the angle formed with the front wall.

Undistinguished, this tree marks the changing seasons. In winter its bare branches are dark, knobbly, stiffly angular. Small, pale green leaves mark the spring. In summer its verdure is a pleasant sight against the grey stone. Briefly in autumn its shed leaves form a circle around it, a scattering of gold on green grass.

Fourth: The Tenement Room

An Edinburgh tenement finishes, at one corner, at a sharp angle. In an upper flat in that corner is a very small room. At one time it held a bed and nothing more. Even the door must open outwards.

Now, under the wide high window, a shelf of blond wood fills the angle of the corner and curves round against the wall. This shelf holds the newest Apple Mac monitor-on-a-stem. Smaller triangular shelves holding a few useful and beautiful things fill the corner angle. To the right under the shelf is a cabinet of shallow drawers. The white walls are bare, save for a mirror on the wall behind the chair. The chair is a particularly comfortable swivel one.

The view is of Arthur's Seat. Moment by moment the hill changes as sunshine and clouds pass over it. Spears of rain fall. Cloud shadows float across it. Sometimes mist covers it. A white covering of snow completely changes its appearance.

Fifth: The Writing Room

All the partitions have been taken down on the east side of the attic. Out of the three small rooms, the passage along them, and the slightly larger room at the south end, one long room has been made. It is quiet at the top of the house.

Three good-sized square windows are inset in the sloping coombe upper wall. They, and the rather low ceiling, the almost cream walls and the brightly variegated patterns of the curtains, make the room cosy. Under each window a table is placed with an upright chair to one side. At night each table has its own light.

The door is in the long wall opposite the south window. The chair at the table by that window is almost an easy chair. On the wall to the right of the door is a low bookshelf holding a few books, mostly reference books.

Each table serves a different purpose. The one at the south end is for sitting, resting, drinking a cup of coffee, or sometimes just for half-dreaming in the sun. On the middle table is a handsome computer. The wide one at the north end is good for spreading out books and papers.

One table has a locked drawer in which to keep journals.

A Close Relationship

Claudine Meyer

I knew something was happening this morning when she took the suitcase out of the upstairs cupboard. She looked a bit pale and I could tell that she was agitated. She packed quite mechanically; she is used to it. She swept the floor and cleaned the sink, emptied out the fridge, making sure that nothing would be left to rot. Then she sat down in front of the television. I could see that she could not concentrate properly. I know her by now; we have quite a strong bond.

When they go they never forget to leave open the shutters of a couple of windows so I can see out. On one side 180 degrees of pure nature: forest, a castle ruin, and magnificent sunsets. And a garden all to myself. No sharing. I can even see the first tee across the way, so it's quite lively. The views over the Lubéron are stunning. I love the bluish hue. Apparently painters like it there. No painting is done here though, not yet. A few reproductions on the walls, nothing special.

The first time they left me I had a terrible fright. It was in August last year. They moved lots of stuff out, all their own private bits and pieces and the good ornaments. They locked up and disappeared. I was really scared. Then a few days later the door opened and a bunch of complete strangers came in: a family of five – two parents and three children. I worried that they would not take care of me and would break whatever was left around but they were fine. I got used to them, their music, her perfume, their laughter. And then after four weeks, they packed their bags and left. By that time I was really confused. Who were these people and who would come next?

Luckily a few days later the usual folks re-appeared. In no time we were all back to normal, clothes back in the cupboards, ornaments in their usual places.

They leave me regularly and I am used to it, nearly. Nor am I completely on my own. The swimming pool attendant comes once a week and the gardener too. They are good-looking young men. Sometimes Jacques comes in with workmen or visitors, bringing fresh air and entertainment.

They did not conceive me. They adopted me. Other people had done all the groundwork before they arrived, Monika, Jacques and his team. It did not take them long to pick me from the seven of us. I overheard them saying they liked me best because I was different, not as square as the others, just what they wanted. I felt rather proud of that. I liked them too, right away, when they came into the office and spoke to Monika. They seemed like happy people, not pretentious, but comfortable and dynamic. I took one look at them and I knew that was it. I wanted Monika to be enthusiastic, but not over keen. I wanted her to inspire trust, and convince them that she recognised quality when she saw it. I wanted her to show them her honesty. Miraculously she did all that. I was so excited I could barely listen to all the questions.

But they wanted to think about it. Think about it! And what if someone else wanted to have me? I had made up my mind. It had to be them.

They came back the following week. I could see she was hiding her excitement. He was very businesslike: serious, thorough, focused. Monika said little, Claudine translated. The men negotiated. Then they shook hands. I loved watching them burst into laughter. And I was so happy I wanted to laugh out loud too.

And so they watched me grow from infancy into adulthood, checking that I was well through and through. It took a whole year. They came to visit regularly, making sure everything was OK. They knew very little about building work but they trusted Jacques and so did I. It was not altogether smooth, but Jacques did his best. At times when he was very angry I shook right down to the foundations. They never knew this, though.

Then everything was finished, inside and out. I was complete – paint, roof, plumbing, heating. I was ready! I could not wait to welcome them – which I did with open arms. He even carried her over the threshold, my threshold. I shed a tear.

They wanted me to look my best so they added the finishing touches. We fit well, them and I. I am so grateful for the care and love they have invested in the way I look. And they have worked so hard. Occasionally I hoped she could calm down, take a breather, give me a chance to settle in myself. But she worked on relentlessly. And he was wise enough to do what he was asked. The beds came in, the sofas, tables and then mountains of stuff from the shops, from towels to wooden spoons. She had done so much planning that in no time at all, I was equipped.

I like the décor very much. Soft orange tones: warm and comfortable. Nothing is flashy, nor too expensive but gentle, earthy, safe, soft, well balanced, and cosy.

41

I must admit I played a trick on her. She could not decide what to do with the bedroom. She would even go to sleep at night thinking about it. There was something about the room which she did not like, but what? Yet I knew the answer. Only I kept her waiting, knowing that one day I would finally tell her. And I did. It was a gorgeous, still, sunny day. She was watching the reflection of the landscape outside in the mirror when she suddenly exclaimed, 'that's it!' She was thrilled. She rushed out to get some green bedside tables, a couple of country wardrobes and lots of fresh flowery bed linen and some bits and pieces in raffia. So pretty! A few bows here and there for the final touches and there it was. A delightful bedroom. No more moaning! Roy likes it too, or so he says. I suspect he just agrees most of the time, to keep the peace.

She is good at shopping. On market days she rushes out and comes back laden with beautiful food, vegetables, lot of fruit, fresh fish, olives and different kinds of bread. I love watching their delight when they eat. She cooks simply, tastily, I guess, because the smells linger. Lovely! I watch her prepare her colourful dishes. She is very creative. She opens the bags, the fridge, the cupboards and puts together ingredients without even looking at recipe books! Then they sit on the patio and spend ages there. I hear the 'hmms!' and the 'ahs!' Sometimes I don't know if it is about the food, or the sun, or the warmth, or all of it. Whatever it is they love it and so do I.

These days we have lots of music around here, all kinds, very loud; it makes me feel like dancing. They do sometimes, tangoing round the lounge. I see them, a bit ridiculous, but funny. They think no one is watching. And when they are not having fun alone, visitors pour in. They occupy the upstairs rooms, kids, young people, older people, some foreigners like him. All sorts. The neighbours come in for drinks and nibbles. And we have parties too.

Last October they gave one party especially for me, to celebrate and consecrate my arrival, and our association, like a wedding or even a blessing. It was lovely. People came; all for me. They called it a housewarming party. And I did feel warm from top to bottom. I am a bit vain; I like compliments, I like to hear that I am beautiful.

The night before the party I overheard her tell a few people that she had a strong feeling that her mother was around, blessing us all . It was very moving and quite spooky. Her mother had died three years before, leaving a little money for her and her children. The inheritance had been settled long ago but unbeknown to her the solicitor had kept a small sum of money for legal reasons. It had arrived that very morning in the form of a cheque, totally unexpected.

I am still growing, not in size, of course, but in maturity. And I am bilingual. I have to be, otherwise I would not understand what they say most of the time; French and English, that is me. We even have UK television. I wish I knew a magician here who would turn on the TV when they leave me behind!

They have some more work to do, the pair of them. When I want new ornaments, new shelves, I let them know, a wink here or a nod there. Somehow they seem to hear me and that is good because although it may sound mundane, I like tidiness. I team well with the garden, the plants and the trees, and I am not going to let them rest on their laurels. She never forgets my suggestions, although she can nag a bit. When she wants something she needs to go out and get it right away. Nothing stops her. Roy escapes to the golf course. He simply loves it. He accumulates trophies. He is so proud of them. Unfortunately they are not always beautiful. She and I agree that he deserves to have them displayed. So we put up with them. One of them looks like a funeral urn. It's not of course but in the dark of a winter night I might have nightmares about it. I'll take care of them but not the urn. I'll leave that alone.

They have gone away, again.

I waved goodbye in my own way, sending them my love. I don't like being left alone at all. I never know when they are going to return. They have kept some clothes in the cupboards and some food in the kitchen. They have even made up the bed, which is a good sign. But still I have no idea how long I will have to wait. Occasionally I peer over their shoulders when they book their flights on the computer so that I have a date for their return but this time it will have to be a surprise. It's November and I am cold. The nights are long and the mistral chills me to the bones. They have left a fire ready for next time, the wood neatly organised, fire-lighters and matches at the ready. All very promising signs. But right now, with the fire un-lit and the overwhelming silence, I feel lonely.

Still, I can look after myself. They'll be back. I know.

Glen Rosa

Ajak

Living things on me walking strolling skipping, my tears rush around my form from many outlets. Running river lets spread as wind blows through every nook and cranny refreshing me. In my watery space there is the gathering of the needy all making space. There's a pecking order, no courtesy here. I can be harsh and rough wild on my blue days. When the yellow sun shines I will burst with life – sharing.

Soft paper, a letter dropped, its vulnerable fibres float through the glen on a blustery day and stick to a tree taking on its textured form, and the wind holds it there. A force spreads it out square. Pink love letter losing its message, thrown away, discarded. It suddenly drops towards the muddy earth and flutters, hovers.

Fool, ill prepared for the trouble I will give her, smooth trainers on her feet hah she's in trouble a silky blouse and shorts God I've seen it all now. She's going to climb, no, slip. Oh yes she'll lose her grip on loose boulders, slither down and scrape her legs. She might even tumble down and bang her uncovered head. Dumb. She's dumb, that fair-skinned lady and in for trouble, taking me on ill-prepared.

Written immediately after a guided visualisation in which writers were invited to fuse their subjectivity with that of a chosen place, and write from its point of view.

The Ruins

Paula Cowie

The ruins lay bare, embraced by the wind daily. Nothing to hide. Let everyone see what went on. Breezes loosen the debris. Howling gales rip out another piece of stone, another piece of history. Another challenge for the weeds' persistence.

The day she found the place was kind. Sunny. Warm. The merest hint of a south-easterly had her tugging her cardigan around her small waist.

She walked slowly towards the central ruin, seeing the village that once was in her mind's eye. Her feet led her through the grass to a doorway. A huge grey lintel lay by her bare feet. Her skin felt its age and the many stories it had to tell. As she sat down, her hands cupped its worn edges; the dryness surprised her.

Drawn back to the moisture of the grass she combed her fingers through its silky blades and heard herself humming an unfamiliar tune. Her eyes closed on the day and she let the images come to her.

Rag-rugging by the fire, children sleeping side by side. Her memories were stilled by the sun's appearance from behind the clouds. The warm September rays shone down on a piece of the earth where she belonged.

We had been writing about landscapes, working from pictures, photographs and memories, concentrating on detailed description. Writers were asked to place a figure in the landscape and to find a connection between the two.

My Scotland

Debbie Hind

Having weaved within my soul
many loose threads of Scottishness,
I now find myself nestling in the urban belt
tied up in incongruent linguistic knots.

Though Aberdeen once was home
fit like wis that?
Highland and lowland divides mingle through me,
gentle and rough yet not completely my own.

Immersed in Gaidhlig voices
which ring around my home
I know their rhythms
but not their whole meaning.

And I hear my ain voice suppressing itsel
to be understood.
Thinking in Scots
Speaking in Northern English.

Ye ken whit ?
Its confusing
fae a Sassenach lassie
eh?

Rain-swept Streets

Tom Britton

The city weeps with rain; empty streets surround me. This is my place, my city. Suddenly I am human again, one against the force of nature. I live for these moments, reclaiming these streets, these rivers of pavement, like a king who has finally claimed his inheritance. I love the look in the eyes of the non-believers when they spot me in my kingdom. All they see is a rain-soaked fool cut adrift like a drunken Noah in search of his ark. Cities are soulful places: to walk in them is to worship in the open, to reconnect with yourself, exposed to the elements.

Crone Tree

Ann Vilen

I called it the Crone Tree, a secret name known only to me. She stood with her rag tag branches and her great trunk and her showering leaves on the edge of Cowhee Mountain, at the end of a dirt road, where a trailer had been removed, leaving nothing but the plumbing sticking up from the ground and the concrete steps. It was an ugly site, mud-rutted, old tins in the weeds, but I was drawn to it by the old crone.

No-one could hear me there, shouting into the wind, swearing, crouching under that tree for a good cry. She became a kind of friend, old and wise, stern but forgiving. Sometimes, looking at the pale sky scalloped by the Blue Ridge in the distance, down to the green valley below, the shadows of her branches would dance over me. I could feel her hands on my shoulders. Shadows like the lightest touch of fingertips and leaves the shape of teardrops falling. I am a woman forever looking up into branches, marvelling at how they can let themselves go in ways that I find impossible.

Centred

Barbara Stone

My shallow, laboured breathing warms the cool air around me, as I stand alone on the roof of the Earth. I am dizzy just taking in the scenery around me, white peak upon white peak, giants compared to my small insignificant being. Overcome by a lack of oxygen, my limbs feel heavy when I try to move, and the light-headedness in my mind passes through pleasure into hallucination.

I draw in a deep breath as I slide into the Earth's folds, gasping in awe at the many colours flashing before me: greys and grey-veined rocks, red and yellow sandstone, brown soils and black metamorphic rocks. I feel smothered by the heaviness of the rock above me, crushing the air from my lungs. I am sinking, the life force pushed out as the rocks tear my flesh bare. Gravity pulls me under, beneath the earth's surface, drowning me in a sea of red and orange lava, the birthing pool of the mountain. I hold my breath.

Down, down and down again into the darkness. No need for air. Here is safety and security. Here is the dark centre of the earth. I am grounded in the core of solid rock. I am centred.

sense

touch

music

scent

image

colour

light

sense

Helen:

Creativity is stimulated in surprising ways when all the senses, not just the dominant visual one, are engaged. We do a lot of exercises that emphasise how writing is a physical, embodied experience; and how a more spontaneous and less censored kind of writing is produced when it is embarked upon from a relaxed, bodily-aware state. Beginning with both movement and stillness, we use all our senses and a range of expressive forms to release writing. We walk around the room, in silence, or guided by music, in order to experience place with our whole being; to attune ourselves to our own personal rhythms in preparation for transmitting them into words on paper, and to access real or imagined distant places as locations for writing. We resist coming to words too early by making collages or producing drawings and paintings of images that have formed during relaxation or visualisation exercises. The 'raw' writing that results from such apparently effortless receptivity to a wide range of sensory stimuli is frequently fresh, original, energetic. Practised and developed over a longer period of time, this approach can help to expand a writer's thematic and stylistic range. Work initiated by these tools and methods therefore also appears in the other sections, but here we give just a few examples of writing produced quickly, within the group. Ideally this work needs to be presented in conjunction with its non-linguistic stimuli, so these pieces require a little explanation, but we hope their inclusion will give some sense of the possibilities of using multi-artform, multi-sensory starting-points.

Lynn:

An acute awareness of all our senses pervades all the writing in this anthology. There are times when writing about sound or taste or scent is a relaxing, inspiring way to begin, or an opportunity to cut loose from difficult personal experience. Sometimes I deliberately break a long run of intense, introspective writing by adding in a session which is lighter and simpler. Just write about the colour blue, I may say, or the sensation of lightness. I play beautiful music and use therapeutic touch to help writers soften and sink into a more sensuous place where they can immerse themselves in imagining rain-drops on their faces, the sound of waves breaking, the scent of vanilla, the touch of a child's hand.

Because I also work as a stained glass artist, I sometimes take in pieces of textured, coloured glass and place them in the window so that the light streams through them. I offer a rainbow and invite writers to choose the colours which match their mood, or ask them to create a picture or sculpture with a number of different pieces. I might use hot and cold colours, light and dark pieces, clear and opaque shapes. Or I may choose a band of colour such as pink through to purple, or combinations of blue, turquoise and green, asking writers to imagine the colour of someone's eyes, the first ring they ever wore, a flower found in a field somewhere.

Musk

Hazel MacPherson

The misty morning hung thick as candy floss;
It had descended quickly from the coast.
I pick out my footsteps carefully,
Imagining where I am. In muffled silence all around
I can smell musk – it could be the moss underfoot –
Or maybe some earthy root.
A sound startles me; I whirl around.
I peer through the grey cotton wool
Then rest on a boulder in the ground:
I will wait until this silky curtain lifts,
Sitting with all my senses as my host.
I am alone; I am alert and in control:
I cannot be found, for I am not lost.

Guided by their sense of touch, everyone selected an unseen item from a bag, and examined it by engaging their other senses. The information gleaned was then used in a piece of writing which did not necessarily or explicitly relate to the original object. Hazel MacPherson selected a silk scarf; Judith Fox, in the following piece, a measuring tape.

Measure

Judith Fox

Why would I want to measure tape?
What will I use this tape for?
How far will I go?
What lengths will I go to?
Will I stay the distance?
Will I come full circle?
What justice, what punishment will be measured out?
Do I measure up?
The full nine yards or a four minute mile?
The straight and narrow:
There are two sides to everything, and in black and white,
But a straight line isn't the shortest distance between two points.

Tape worms and inch worms,
Feet but no hands,
The hare and the tortoise – Zeno's paradox
If I travel half the distance I'll still have half way to go.
Can I meet myself in the middle
Coming back?

Sarah

Ajak

Sarah. Even my name is something I abhor. Sarah: soft, Biblical, old-fashioned. This name doesn't represent who I am. I am Alex. Alex is strong, serious, solid. Not that I want a sex change. I'm boyish: a tomboy who always wanted to climb trees.

On another occasion the group was provided with drawing materials, and each member quickly sketched someone else in the room. Then we folded up the results and placed them in the bag. Everyone pulled out a portrait and wrote about the character depicted, without attempting to relate it to the original subject. Accurate drawing skills were not necessary — indeed the most interesting results occurred where the image appeared to be of a different age, or sex, to the original.

Slow Movements: Rock-Bound Inlets

M R McDonald

Rock-bound inlets aglint with the sea's lapping and ebbing. The depth of clear green water observed through rippling sand. Tangled seaweed draped over seaward sloping surfaces. The pervasive peace of a boat-moored bay. The calm of invited contemplation — soft light and reflections.

This, and the next piece, are responses to the slow movement of a Beethoven string quartet. Participants were asked, 'if this music were a sound-track to a film, what kind of scene would it accompany?'

Slow Movements: Empty

Ajak

He left her.

She watched in silence as he walked along the grass verge towards the hills. Inside, her heart was heavy, and the pain of emptiness was a gaping hole in her centre. As his figure became smaller and smaller, she became aware of every part of her body. Heavy hands hung like great boulders at her side, her face was drawn down, gravity was pulling her whole being, and if the ground had opened she would willingly have lain down in the space. It started to rain. Tears fell as he disappeared from her life forever. She had forced him to make a decision, forced him to be strong. She turned towards their cottage, empty from that moment on.

Never fill again, never fill again, and never fill again.

Looking for Someone

Felicity Milne

The darkness is all around me, intense, deep. I feel no sense of being; I think perhaps that in this darkness I do not exist at all. I am numbed by the thick blackness, as it envelops and consumes me. I hear my breath and within it, the sound of fear. If I am aware of any thing else at all, it is of my own smallness.

A tiny spot has now appeared in the distance. It shines out at me, a fragment of light in this black place. It's not red or yellow but honey coloured, just like a drop of pure honey, waiting to be tasted. I am approaching, slowly, mesmerised by its temptation. If I touch it, what will happen?

I can't resist; I must put just one finger on this liquid amber.

I am reaching forward in the darkness, my eyes focused on the spot.

I am now touching it gently with the tip of one finger. It's as if I am pressing an electrifying button and my senses are suddenly alerted as adrenaline takes over. The effect is astonishing; the amber honey spot is expanding like liquid gold, getting larger and larger. The spot is now so expanded that it has become a tunnel of bright swirling colours, now large enough for me to crawl through on my hands and knees.

Should I enter? I am not sure if I have the courage.

I am peering cautiously into the tunnel. Looking about, it's beautiful, surrounding me with the most fantastic glow of moving light, honey amber, bronze and flecks of orange, which are warming me after the darkness and compelling me to enter and move on. I am suddenly revived and full of hope. I am not thinking of my doubts and fears any more: they are behind me, cast away in the black place.

I am moving forward slowly, carefully, in the vibrant light. I feel stronger, braver. I am gradually gaining confidence.

The end of the tunnel is just a short distance up ahead. If I reach it, I should be able to stand tall. Will I find what I have been looking for: the real me, the one that got left behind too many years ago; the one that is everybody else's someone?

This, and the following five pieces, were inspired by the colours of stained glass: hot reds and oranges and cool blues and greens.

Kingfisher

Barbara Stone

The electric blue of feathers flitting over the water veers towards the air. There the feathers mingle with the blue flashes of forked lightning in the threatening sky. As forks reach the earth their natural power transforms into human power, the blue veins of royalty, whose blood flows over the land and drains out into the sea. The water vapour rises, uniting again with the kingfisher as he swoops down to earth in his search for sustenance.

A carpet of woodland blue-bells surrounds the kingfisher, an unnatural habitat for food. He flaps his wings in confusion, blue on blue, until he sees them – the deep blue eyes of his mother, smiling warmly at him – transforming his confusion to joy. Joy quickly turns to sorrow as the blue becomes the colder, paler blue of death. He can't move; he lies shivering with cold, trembling at his own weakness. His fear threatens him, paralysing him so he can't escape, until he sees his salvation, the sight of the blue moon.

On the wings of joy, powered by the magnetism and mystery of the moon, he veers again then carefully descends, flittering over the water. From the surface he snatches his fish, and flies away into the darkness of his sanctuary, his hiding place, under the bridge.

Blue

Elke Williams

Bright blue ribbons are waving
Light blue waves are lapping
Dark blue ink is resting
In a blue bowl

It lets you see what is in your mind:
What's in your mind is everywhere.

Red

Elke Williams

Cold, brown and quite dead:
Broken off branches, discarded wood,
Old chairs, an old door, a thrown away shed.

Yellow, bright and very hot:
Sparks, noise, power – the lot!
Energy bursting from one spot!

Red and glowing,
Flames like tongues
Reaching for more

More food, more air,
More, more, more!
Tongues retract and

Silent heat,
Spreading through you,
Makes you stay.

Firelight

Helga T Thomson

I am a child visiting our neighbour's house. It is a dark basement flat. It is a cold flat but it is filled with warmth for me. I am in the living room, sitting on the stone hearth. I stare at the black and empty grate. Mrs Daniels has just cleaned the ashes out, piling them first into thick newspaper sheets, wrapping the grey dust up tight and putting them in the bin outside the front door.

I wish I could light a new fire.......she lets me! I get newspaper, roll the double sheet up into a long column and tie a knot in it. The tubular paper will quickly take light.

I get fire-lighters; break them in two – the crumbs smell of paraffin. It is all over my hands and I can smell its oily texture.

The newspaper print takes light quickly. The black ink burns blue and orange and yellow and white. It is fascinating but sad – the big flame won't last.

It will help the coals, though. They take long to ignite and start to glow. Yellow and blue dances between black and orange.

I stare at the flames and see different people, pictures and images – or do I? Do I look for them because I have been told they are there?

I want to touch the fire but of course I don't.....I have been warned not to.

Candlelight

Helga T Thomson

There are live, warm candle flames in a church. Little lights dancing for God ... or a Saint ... or a Statue of Our Lady ... or whoever smiles down. You pay 20p for a little tea light or a miniature candle. You must never blow out anyone else's candle flame. It would negate your own. The wax drips down as your wish is granted. It makes a mess. Ladies who clean the church scrape it off vigorously. It is a lot of work but they say, 'sure, if you didn't do it for God, who would you do it for?' The church is dark but many candles burn. The flames are transparent at the bottom. The flame is oval and the dancing fire is blue, surrounded by a yellowy, white, ivory halo.

It is Christmas and we have an Adventkranz. You burn one red candle a week. One of the four tall, fat, red candles on a ring of thick, leafy pine needles. They look funny. First one out of the four, then two out of the four, then three out of the four get small. First three stay tall, then only two stay tall, then only one stays tall. The stubs are unbalanced against the height of the other candles. They show how the candle is really white with a red wax surround. Red wax is a cover; white wax is the centre – what a fraud! I wanted the candles to be all red – not just a pretend red. I feel cheated. I am aggrieved and irritated. I do not think I like the Adventkranz too much anymore.

I Wish

M R McDonald

I wish the Autumn foliage would change colour slowly
I wish the sun would light voluminous clouds all day
I wish the roses would bloom unruffled by the wind
I wish the rain would drench the parched grass
I wish the moon would be full and clear with light
I wish the Autumn berries would keep coming to ripeness
I wish the day would yield happy events, more and more
I wish the silence for thought could be all-pervading
I wish the twilight would remain, serene
I wish the cool grass on my bare feet would meet my joy
I wish laughter would be my good fortune

A line-poem written immediately after a progressive relaxation and guided visualisation exercise.

challenge

transition

pain

illness

disruption

disability

isolation

conflict

fear

loss

demons

challenge

Helen:

Therapeutic writing groups provide a dedicated space for the linguistic exploration of problems and difficulties; health and relationship issues; pain, loss, grief . . . from the past and the present. Inevitably, personal experience also colours work produced in groups which do not have such a 'therapeutic' slant: boundaries between therapeutic and more literary writing are often indistinct and overlapping. The expression of feelings in a way that is personally authentic, accurate and meaningful can be a very healing process; further healing and change occur when the language of personal expression is transformed and crafted into poetry or fiction. The pieces included here cover both stages of this process.

Lynn:

Many of those who are attracted to our writing classes and workshops are dealing with personal issues which range from the niggling and annoying to the hugely challenging. Because of what they have been through, or are still enduring, their antennae can be super- sensitive and their skins paper-thin. These walking wounded people astonish me with their courage. They come to translate their experiences into words, share their ideas and feelings with others, ask for validation, and write their truths so that they are there in black and white, allowing them to move on. One writer said, 'I have this heavy ruck-sack on my back and it's full of stuff I need to shed.' Into my groups come victims of abuse, people with eating disorders, mental health problems and chronic physical illness; people who have suffered bereavement, the loss of a partner or child, or who feel lost themselves. They may be at a cross-roads, unsure of which way to turn, or they may be experiencing a loss of self-confidence or a sense of malaise that they have not yet put into words.

Being given permission to write about illness and distress in a way which truly reflects personal experience is essential for anyone whose experiences have been dismissed and trivialised by the medical profession, by others in authority or even by family and friends. They are left searching for a mirror which reflects their own reality and they find it in the nodding heads around the table and the voices which say, 'I know. I understand. I have been there too.' I watch writers grow and blossom. Masks which they have worn for years to protect themselves from an insensitive society come down in the Writing Room because here they find compassion.

I am aware that I walk a tight-rope between gently nudging people towards expressing themselves and allowing them to hold back when they come up against a barrier which they are not yet ready to cross. One way of resolving this is to introduce neutral topics and starting points, which can be coloured lightly or darkly with emotion. Once I showed my writing critique group a series of abstract photographs of a tartan scarf – left lying in a snowy field, caught on brambles, at the bottom of tenement stairs. From these pictures came Claudine Meyer's 'Murray's Death', in which the scarf appears briefly in a single line, and Tom Britton's 'Bunnet and Scarf', which is the story of the death of the writer's grandfather.

Frozen in Time

Maureen Lockhart

I am seven
I am sitting on a log on a grassy bank
Waiting
I am waiting for the other children to find the ball

I turn to look through my living-room window
See my parents quarreling behind glass
My mother cries
My father shouts
Behind the glass

I don't hear what they are quarreling about
But I understand my father's anger
Feel my mother's distress
Like a photograph
Frozen in time
I am outside
Waiting

Later when my father is gone
My mother has broken down
No-one explains
I am outside
Waiting
Waiting to hear what is to become of me

I am at my grandmother's house
In a row of peas
Sweet-peas in profusion climb the ends of the rows
The sweet sour taste of nearly ripe strawberries in my mouth

I wait among the rows of raspberry canes

Sampling everything
Raw peas black and red currants
Poignant flavours of remembrance
Of a time of waiting
Outside of time

Precious Food

Elke Williams

Feeding time
Joyous time
Blissful time
Peaceful time?

Warm sweet smell
Tempting smell
Seducing smell
Captivating smell?

Warm food
Mashed up food
Nourishing food
Precious food?

And here she comes –
Provider of warmth and food
And love and affection?
Centre of the world!

I sit on her knee
Don't hold me so tight!
My arm behind
Under her arm and on her back

I am only small!
My other arm down by my side
Don't grip me so hard
Now I can't move

Here comes the spoon
No time to waste
And another
No time to waste
And another
Why all the haste?

I have enough
No more for me
My mouth is full
Don't want to eat

A hand grips my nose
Now I can't breath
Have to swallow
Down it goes

73

I am so full now
But can not speak
I am only little
I am weak

Precious food
Has to be eaten
There's no choice
There's no pleasure and no delight

Why?

Sandwich

Stephanie Taylor

I look at the fridge.

Don't look.

I stare through the TV and smoke.

I glance at the cupboard.

Don't glance.

I stare back through the TV and smoke. My eyes go to the cupboard again and my body follows. I will just have a small sandwich. Bread, no butter. Thin, thin cheese and pickle: I don't want to undo the good done at the gym this morning, but everybody eats dinner, don't they? That can't hurt. The body needs fuel. I pop a slice of cheese into my mouth before I finish making the sandwich and have to cut another to replace it. By the time I sit down with the plate on my knee I've made the decision. Just once more, then I *promise* I will be done with this filth. I squeeze the rest of the sandwich into my mouth and wash it down with diet coke. I go to make another. Toasted thick bread this time with lashings of butter. I'm not shy about slicing the cheese either, one for me, one for my sandwich. I add mayo, pickle, tomatoes and mashed potato.

The guilt starts but there is no going back now. I need to satisfy this urge.

Learner

C MacLaverty

When she wasn't doing laundry at the hospital,
Christine Grindy taught me to drive
on our horseshoe island:
a land without traffic lights or a roundabout.
She took no money, but listed previous gifts of thanks:
a fine china tea set, gold jewellery (24 carat), a radio cassette.

She could have been 43 or 53, as slight as me;
both of us toy-like within the rusting hulk of a Passat Estate,
doing 20 on empty roads, watched only by
chewing, camel faced sheep.

We drove to visit her sister,
bed bound and bandana-ed in a back room that needed air.
'The cancer,' volunteered Christine, fastening her seat belt.
'I'm sorry,' I said, not knowing what to say.
She wiped tears from her creased face.
'Mirror, Signal, Manoeuvre,' she said.
'Don't you forget.'

It's spring and my head feels like a helium balloon.
When I step shaking from the car
the examiner's already striding away.
And suddenly, here's Christine,
standing alone on the corner of Main Street
with hands thrust into anorak pockets.
As I throw my arms around her neck,
her small frame keeps its stiffness
and in the elated crash of the moment,
nothing compares to this.

Overlooked

C MacLaverty

I refuse to put up net curtains or Venetian blinds.
Lying in bed, my gaze falls on cement-coloured sky.
I drink in the January daylight,
vacant and flat as a day old glass of water.

Through the bare trees, fluorescent light
glows sallow from your windows.
I see flickering computer screens,
wipe-clean memo boards,
an occasional bald man wearing glasses.
I can almost smell the photocopier;
sense the quiet comfort
that comes with everyday purpose.

Can any of you see me?
I suspect my body is clearer than my face;
the daily ramp under the duvet,
a forearm glimpsed by the bedside lamp.
It's been years. I'm embarrassed; I want to explain.
I don't care; I shouldn't have to explain.

I wait for May's leaves to unfurl once more;
the explosion of green that keeps us obscured from each other.
I will throw open my top floor window and lie
in a carpeted pool of sunlight.
Summer will smell sweet on my limbs
and only birds and airplanes will see my naked skin.

Buried

Mandy Calder

'Sorry! sorry! sorry!' she mumbles, begging forgiveness from the hordes of passers-by who carelessly bump into her as she tries to slide unnoticed through the bustling crowd. It is unusual to see her in such a busy place: she normally tries to avoid the city centre. On the few occasions when we spoke she seemed nervous and her voice was barely audible even though we were in an empty park. I sense that she would rather be in that quiet park today or, rather, still in the comfort of her own home. She does not appear at ease among people. It is as if each individual she encounters poses a personal threat.

Strangers to her world cannot fail to see her frailties, her thinness obvious despite the layers of baggy clothes under which she attempts to hide. The uneasiness she feels covers her like a familiar cloak, one she is permanently unwilling to shed. They may wonder if she is ill and with what disease she is afflicted, the way we are all adept at labelling anything we find hard to deal with. She could be described as 'different' to relieve the observer of the need for further classification.

Despite her shyness and her trepidation she manages to articulate her feelings well. I sense that she is actually a very strong woman, though I know she would be surprised to hear this. During our conversations she has struck me as bitterly honest and open, as well as having immense insight into what is hurting her. This pain must be extremely personal, as she tries to protect herself and to remain in control at all times: she never cries or raises her voice in anger or despair. Yet her body language betrays her. Vulnerability screams from her pores as if the little girl that she once was is pleading to be seen.

I find myself wondering what has happened in her life to make her so afraid and so suspicious. I have yet to see her laugh freely: she is always guarded and on edge, and when a smile does cross her lips her eyes remain blank. When we talked, she whispered to me of how lonely she felt and how isolated she was. I remember asking her what she enjoyed doing. It was then and only then that she looked me straight in the eye as she quietly muttered, 'nothing. Nothing brings me joy.' I knew at once she was speaking her truth: she did not look capable of inventing a lie. It was as if merely surviving each day drained her of all her energy and strength.

I choose to follow her as she weaves her way through this packed street, offering apologies every few seconds. Her step is quick; she must be anxious for this ordeal to be over. Yet, as she is unfamiliar with the ways of the crowd, she makes little progress. This seems to be the theme of her life: impatience driving her forwards whilst immense pain keeps her rooted in her past. She keeps her eyes fixed on the ground so that she does not have to confront an onlooker's gaze – that would be too intimidating.

An overwhelming sadness engulfs me as I continue to trace this intriguing woman's path. I yearn to reach out to save her, the idea of rescuing her masking my own needs. The impotence I see before me is a painful reminder of my own infirmities and the dark spots of which I am hugely afraid. Yet the woman does not scare me. Surprisingly, she consoles some part of me; the part, no doubt, deep within, that seeks constant illumination about the essence of being real. Her frailty offers me some guide to the rough texture of the human spirit and I am immensely grateful for this insightful mapping of territory as yet unknown.

I sense that if I explained how she allowed me a rare moment of self-realisation, she would think it was I that needed to be saved. How then do I find the words to reach out to her and to show her both my compassion and my appreciation? I am in awe of her hidden strength and wish only that she was aware of her vitality. She inhabits such a dark space and I fear that is impeding her vision. Her world is void of any sign of the lighter sides of life: she is forever in the wake of a shadow. Yet today, in this busy street, it is I who tread gently in her shadow.

When it is too difficult or painful to write directly about oneself using the first person, adopting the third person allows the writer a bit more distance and objectivity, enabling her to function as an observer. Mandy Calder plays with this technique with great ingenuity.

There is Always an Angel

Rose

I am handed an envelope. In it is £100, my passport, a divorce summons and a statement from my husband saying that from now on I am denied all access to my four year old son. My child has been abducted by his father and I have no idea where he has gone.

It is like an execution. I am humiliated and betrayed, discarded, abandoned and nullified. It is a death, depriving me of my role as a loving mother, now and forever.

In my youth and naivety, I married the man I thought I wanted to be with. My feelings were honest and true, if hopelessly innocent. Love was blind. There was something about this man which attracted me, as if deep under all his repressed and negative being there was a good person who needed to be loved and accepted most of all by himself. I believed that.

So begins Rose's long, distressing story in which a son is taken away from his mother. The narrative stretches to 5000 words and is too long to include here in its entirety, but the extracts below give some understanding of her plight, her despair and her never ending attempts to find her child, to hold on to hope, and to re-build her life.

As I was to find out, my husband could neither receive nor give love. His had been a dysfunctional childhood in which material possessions were plentiful but love seemed absent. I think he did not know what love was. And as time passed within the marriage, I understood that I was the under-dog. When I spoke, it was if I were talking to the wall. I was the one who had to adapt and change. I was his door-mat. I was trapped. I tried to breathe life into a living death. I overlooked my own needs and succumbed to the most extraordinary life in a big house, a mansion, isolated in the country, left to myself weekend after weekend while he played his golf, his snooker. I was living in a foreign land, alone in the middle of nowhere, learning to accept a situation which was beyond belief. Who could I turn to?

Our intimate relationship was non-existent yet on one occasion of togetherness my son was conceived. When I told my husband, he showed little joy. As my pregnancy advanced I found no peace, love or understanding. When the contractions began, it was the doctor who held my hand. 'Talk about something you love,' he said, and I talked about the Swedish summer. He listened. A complete stranger listened, really listened, and I felt his compassion. When my husband came, he just looked at me. 'You can touch her,' the doctor said. My husband looked at me, embarrassed. Later, the doctor offered me the choice of forceps or a Caesarian. 'Don't hurt his head,' I said. And so my baby and I were knocked out, and when I came to again, it was 2am and the nurse brought in my baby. A perfect miracle. An angel of love.

What I did not know was that even then I was being betrayed. My husband, supported by ranks of people who for me were unreal and unapproachable, was planning to be rid of me. My husband's family knew about his plans for divorcing me long before I did.

Rose and her sister spend a celebratory day in London. While she is there, her husband has a package delivered to her hotel. In it is the letter which changes her life.

The next day, in a London hotel, a divorce summons was delivered together with £100 and my passport. I was to return to Sweden. I was to be denied access to my son. I was instructed not to try to find out where he had been taken. My credit card facilities were withdrawn; we had to return the things we had bought.

My sister and I returned to Scotland. I had nowhere to go. The house was shut and I had no keys. We just stood and looked at my house. I was lost and helpless in a situation I was powerless to do anything about. There was no option but to walk away. My sister had to return to Sweden and there I was, completely alone.

And so begins a long legal battle in which her husband uses his wealth, power and influence to strip Rose of everything she owns and to block access to her son. Rose appears in court to hear her personality un-picked and re-invented. There are lies and blackmail. She is described as an unstable, unworthy, useless wife and mother. The outcome is totally in her husband's favour. For the next eleven years her son lives with her husband and paid carers, and if Rose wants to see him she must write a formal letter of request. Every time. And yet Rose slowly rebuilds her life. She finds a flat to rent and begins working.

I had always been interested in health, especially alternative methods of healing. When someone suggested I work in a health shop, it seemed the right decision, giving me a footing in a career which already interested and absorbed me. I worked in that shop for a year, for love. I was not paid. A friend of mine who knew my situation suggested buying somewhere that would become my own shop, somewhere she had spotted. It was meant to be. I managed to buy it by the smallest margin. But still I had nowhere to live because I had exhausted all my financial resources.

But Rose again finds a solution, albeit a temporary one, and so life continues, insecurely, always presenting her with challenges and upheavals. Many years later she has her own shop, her own thriving business and her own flat bought for her by her son's trustees after the death of her husband.

There was also a room at the back of my shop with a cooker and some space, and this became my refuge, a place where I could be myself. It opened on to a small garden which I tended. It was blessed. I felt this space was truly my own because I owned it. In some ways it would have felt good to put a bed in there too because then I would have been completely independent, but it was too small. There, in that very personal space, my business grew, even though often I was working until midnight. I did it – and was successful. For seventeen years I kept my business afloat and I loved it. And it wasn't just a shop. People came in for a bag of flour and opened their hearts to me, telling me their life stories. The place became a haven for healing.

Here are the closing paragraphs of Rose's story.

It has been essential for me to write this. By taking this step towards releasing the past, I can reclaim my true self which is my birthright. Here is the harmony, the balance and the equilibrium that keeps me alive, among the living. Life is for living.

A mother's love for her child is the strongest emotional link on earth. A mother is the most important restorer and protector of life. To brutally break this bond is akin to murder, of the physical, the emotional and the spiritual being. Nothing can justify such a deed, as has been shown in this case.

Today, years on and a lifetime of experience and wisdom later, I can say I AM his loving mother. Now and always. He is my loving son, but because of what happened to him and to me, he is unable to express his feelings towards me. I can leave this world knowing that I have done all I can for him. I can go with peace of mind. There is no more to be done. Life will show him whether he wants to receive or not. It is there for his taking. Only he can decide. At last I need to release him, and all the feelings that hurt me.

My son remains incapable of being natural in my presence. The distance between us grows ever wider. He describes our relationship as dysfunctional. At the moment he lives with his wife and children abroad and we barely communicate. There is the annual politeness of Christmas and birthday cards . He dislikes the phone. He does not write. And so the past repeats itself. To distance myself from my own child, and his children, is heart-breaking. It is as if half of me is alive and half is dead. What is left is time, time to reflect and time to choose what to do. I now leave everything to life itself. Nature brings forth what needs to be. There is always an angel.

Finally there are just the words, 'I just want you to know that deep in my heart I love you.'

Rose has held this story inside herself for most of her life. One of the first writers to come to the Salisbury Centre, she has been part of this group ever since. At first we saw only the Rose she showed to us, the warm, loving woman who wrote about the beauty of nature. It must have been a year before she revealed a bit more about herself. Then one day she wept as she disclosed that her only child had been taken from her. Another year passed while she contemplated committing her story to paper. Finally, together, we sat in front of Lynn's computer screen week after week while she dictated it from start to finish and at last, to use her own words, 'it is out.' Rose says she is relieved to have done this. It has released her.

Threat

Stephanie Taylor

His face darkens, tic toc a big dark clock. The eyes go tic, the eyebrows toc. He leans slowly towards me, neck strained, a vein, a tic, a tic, a toc.

I smell his hot breath. Tic toc, tic toc. Slowly, slowly the big hand reaches three. Three o'clock tic toc, tic toc.

His shadow confuses me, the face obscured. Stuck, I still feel the tic, the tic and the tic toc.

The push and the ticking and the face of the clock, my heart twitches and bleats with a tic, tic, tic, toc.

I Find Myself in the Company of Strangers

Judith Fox

Indigo, sea glass, pewter and steel
Shoulders a slash of burnt orange
Neck a spike of acid yellow

Duck egg blue
Small as a humming-bird's

Deep, deep, deep
Full fathom five
All surface
No depth
Hidden depth
Hidden source
Hidden truth

Layers
Tissue and steel
Rough edges, sharp corners
Brash, flash
Anger is purple
Red is too dangerous

Raven wings, sharp claws, soft underbelly
The centre is fragmented
The centre will not hold
There are no boundaries
No edge, no definition

Where do I start and where do I stop?
Touch is dangerous
I might crumble
You might realise there is nothing underneath

Or, that the whole universe is there
And I am too big, too much, too strong
No compromise, no shadow, no self

I find myself in the company of strangers

Inspired originally by pieces of stained glass. Judith Fox uses colour to explore personal
identity.

She Lay on the Bed

Ajak

She lay on the bed with the covers over her legs and her head was under the pillow, the transparent curtain reflecting clouds on her trim waist. A constantly changing pattern. Changing pattern, yes she will rise up soon. A storm will take over from the soft sunny tranquillity of the morning. She will walk through the day changing mood. Her eyes, many expressions watching, changing from hour to hour, and she'll drift through the castles of her mind, the ruins. She will reflect the ruins, the marks made by her inability to understand words, messages. She will trample and squash. To hold the pillow down hard, strong, would take all my strength. My shadow black and ominous. A creature I don't recognise, black like my thoughts. I set down the breakfast tray and walk away knowing not to make a sound. She will rise when she is ready unlike the sun deep as the ocean and as multilayered. She may smile big and warm or bite like a frost. I never know. If I dared I could lift the pillow and look at the exquisite face at rest, pale clear skin and rosy pink lips. An overdose for her, then me. Stub her out. But the good days what about.....I love her good days.

Gremlin

Elke Williams

I am the owner of a gremlin –
It sits on my back
Looking over my shoulder.
When it is quiet
I don't notice it much –
I feel the weight, though.
When it is active
It pulls me down.
All sorts of people are interested in this creature.
Enquiring about it, asking me.
I don't know who gave it to me
But I am unable to shake it off.
I don't want it anymore.
Someone has even given it a name.
They call it: your mood!
And keep asking,
How is your mood?
It has a personality of its own:
I just seem to be the host.
People keep looking at it
Sitting on my shoulder.

Written after a particularly unhelpful discussion between psychiatrist and patient.

A Day in September

Elke Williams

A day in September and I am walking along the beach. It stretches as far as my eyes can see. The air is mild and there is hardly any wind.

It is warm. I see people walking their dogs or playing golf and in the distance a football game is going on. People are out on their bikes and several of them are cycling past me.

What I like most, though, is the vast open space: a beach as long as you can see, and very far away the sea meeting the sky. I feel compelled to look into the distance, as if I am trying to find the future, to be able to see that the world goes on beyond all the problems which are clouding my view.

I ran away from home. I couldn't stand being in the house any more, felt trapped, wanted to be alone, needed space and that open outlook into the horizon.

I walk and walk, then I sit down, try to read my book but find I can't concentrate. My mind wanders off and I am drawn to look out to sea, a very calm blue sea in the evening sunlight. I ponder what to do but I just can't see the future.

I wish I could carry on walking to that point on the horizon where sky meets land, the blue sky and the golden sand. I don't want to go back to the hotel. I can see it, in the distance, behind me.

Could I stay on the beach? Could I fade away like the sunshine behind the tall trees?

I want my life to end here, like the warm Autumn day, losing warmth and light, drifting into night, getting darker and getting colder.

How long have I been here? It is nearly dark now. I want the world to stop and let me get off. I want a way out. I have been struggling for too long.

Suddenly I realise it is not going to be that easy: the night is too mild for me to drift away on the beach. I feel stupid and cheated.

Would it be a struggle if I went into the water, reaching out to a disappearing horizon, wanting peace, wanting to get away from the misery inside my head? Do I want to find out or am I a coward?

And then I remember my tablets in my hotel room: they could give me sleep. I long for sleep; I need sleep to get away from myself. Reluctantly I get up. I still feel cheated because there is no easy way out for me and I feel very alone.

Falling Through Fall

Judith Fox

This is a bad time of year for me, too many pulls from the past. Overarching and subsuming everything else is the fact that Kevin died at the turning of the year. Autumn has two faces, like Janus looking both ways.

Autumn. September, October send me confused and conflicted messages. My new year, start of academic terms, new beginnings, but also deep, deep loss, loneliness, depression, back breaking, standing on the edge of the chasm and trying to decide whether I will fly if I jump or just fall and keep falling. Falling through the fall with no-one to catch me, no-one to raise me up again. Hitting the bottom I start the painful climb up, but flash floods and earth tremors rock me and set me back, tumbling free-fall, scrabbling and scrambling for hand-holds, hands to hold, ledges and overhangs to provide shelter.

Where were you when your life changed? If you don't know I envy you, because it means you've never had a life changing, defining moment.

We talk about dying for the one we love, but that's wrong, that's the easy bit. The hard way is to go on living without the one you love.

One of us died on that mountain, but I'm not sure which one of us it was. I'm still here but I'm not sure I'm still alive.

You were 23 when you died – but you're still 23 and I am 20 years further away from you.

Somebody stole my life when I wasn't looking. Three months is not enough, not enough to even know what might have been.

Sunrise isn't romantic when you watch it alone, and the phases of the moon meaningless when you cannot be a woman. All the feathers on a bird allow it to fly. A single feather still flies, but it has to go where the wind takes it.

And then I lost my mother. Terribly careless of me really – I've looked in all the drawers and cupboards but I just can't seem to find her anywhere.

Murray's Death

Claudine Meyer

The ads on the radio are futile.
I have a sore tooth but what is a sore tooth compared to their pain?
I don't want to go out. I should; the sun is shining, but I want to stay put.
Stay put and do what?
Read my book, listen to a CD?
This all seems as futile as the ads.
Sleep? I can't. I was awake all night. I can't stop thinking about it.
I can't even cry. My friend Ingrid cried when she heard. I didn't.
A tightness in my belly and my throat comes and goes and I am light-headed.
And I can't cry.
All I can do is think.
I can't just feel my pain, I have to think it, or stop myself thinking it.
I am confused and I don't even allow that.

I can't imagine what they must feel, his parents, his wife, his sister. Like a yo-yo, I put myself in their shoes and out of them as quickly as possible. It could happen to me too, and if it did I know I could not cope, or could I? How are they doing? Is life taking over yet? Are they feeling relief now that the waiting has stopped, just before the grief sets in? Are they keeping busy before Saturday, making arrangements for people arriving from abroad and deciding where they will feed us all afterwards? On Saturday, England and Scotland will meet once more, the rugby pitch a battlefield.

He used to wear a bright red tartan scarf to go to the games, turning into a serious nationalist five afternoons a year.

I stop myself asking God, 'why him?' He was young and beautiful and happy and he was a good man. Why him? Perhaps it was meant, perhaps his soul had been in a body who died at that age before, so he had to. It was written. That sounds quite profound, doesn't it? Only right now, it is not. Nothing is.

This and the next piece were written in response to the same disturbing, abstract photographs of a tartan scarf. We include them side by side to illustrate how the same starting point can trigger very different pieces of writing.

Bunnet and Scarf

Tom Britton

At the traffic lights I saw a leaf fall grey and dry from an empty tree. Winter is when things die. 83 years into his life my Grandfather chose this time to die. It was as if he just decided that he had had enough of living, so he went out for a walk and died. The paramedic fought and fought but my Grandad had made up his mind and there was no coming back. He seemed very wee lying in the ambulance. He had always been a big man in my life with big hands and a big smile.

It was strange how calm I felt when we were racing to the hospital. At one point I was almost tempted to tell them to slow down. He was gone. It was pointless.

As we turned a corner one of his big hands fell off the stretcher. Those hands came to my aid and my protection so many times and here was I placing a dead man's hand back. I didn't really know why. I guess it was just one of the things you do when you are in an ambulance with your dead Grandad.

There was one time when we were up in St. Andrews at my grandparents' caravan when I was a wee boy. The sun was huge and beaming. The wind was strong enough to fly kites. I had many kites but there was one that my Grandad himself would fly. It had a picture of an eagle on it and it would fly higher than anything else. He had attached an old butcher's string to give it that extra length. This day started as any other at the caravan. I got up early and went with my Grandad to get the paper and the morning rolls. We returned and put the kettle on for my Grandmother to have a cup of tea. It was my job to fill up the kettle with water and to put it on the gas ring. My Grandfather then struck a match and lit the gas. I got a tea bag, a cup and the milk from the fridge. My Grandad showed me how to make the tea and I took it through to my Grandmother. After we had had our own breakfast, it was time to get the kites out. I went to the cupboard under the window seat, carefully took out my grandfather's, and handed it to him. Then I went back and took my shorter kite. By the time I got outside my Grandfather already had his kite flying high. I was totally absorbed in watching it soar and dive. Then my Grandfather spoke:

'Would you like to fly it?'

I turned towards him with the same absorbed look on my face and couldn't find any words.

He simply said:

'Here.'

For what seemed like a long couple of seconds the kite continued to soar, but then the wind seemed to sense that I had never flown this kite before. A sudden blast of wind took string and kite out of my hands and out towards the East Sands. I stood frozen, deeply ashamed. Time seemed to stop as I awaited my Grandfather's reaction. When I finally found the courage, I opened my eyes and looked at him. His eyes were still looking towards the Sands. I was expecting an angry voice or a disappointed stare but this silence was beginning to unsettle me. Suddenly he turned towards me and looked, well not really at me, more through me. It was if he sensed the anxiety inside me. His look was a strange and curious mix of forgiveness and questioning, as if he was daring me to forgive myself. He gently rubbed the top of my head and pointed towards the sea.

Wiping away tears from my eyes I suddenly realised that the kite, although still flying high above everything else, had stopped moving out to sea. The long extra string that my Grandfather had added to the kite had got caught somewhere.

We both set off at great speed down through the caravan park and along the path to the East Sands. There in front of us was the kite. The string had caught on a barbed wire fence and was going nowhere. We returned to the caravan in triumph, greeted with cheers and clapping. From that day on my Grandfather's kite was mine.

A hand on my shoulder made me jump as I realised we had now arrived at the hospital. It was the paramedic telling me that he would leave me for a few minutes with him.

Staring at my Grandfather I realised that what he gave me that day was something that could never have been bought for all the gold in the world. He gave me belief in myself. I found myself holding his hand and realised that I had in fact been crying. His hand was still warm and I whispered quietly to him. I could sense the paramedic making quiet noises outside, obviously needing the ambulance for another emergency. It had been kind of him to let me sit here. I turned to my Grandfather for the last time and kissed his forehead. I then picked up his scarf and bunnet and left. There was only one destination for me.

As I walked through the caravan park I realised how barren and lifeless it looked in the winter. I momentarily wondered if this was the right thing to do. I walked down the hill slowly, the fence coming into view. The sun came out just as I reached it. The field beyond the fence was white with frost and suddenly everything seemed perfect. I put the bunnet on a fence post and tied the scarf over the wire, and I remembered. As I stood there a blast of wind came out of nowhere and carried the scarf away across the field. I started to laugh and cry at the same time.

Bonfire

Ernie

"Written after having buried personal papers that belonged to my father, who died two and a half years ago. I was affected by seeing his signature and handwriting disappearing forever. It is intended to be a requiem for my own past as well as my father's memory."

Surreptitously, having waited for twilight to come,
I break the sticks and place them on the wet soil.
Small pieces of paper, aspects of a life now passed.
Carefully stored for decades, waiting for this day.

A light sparks in the gathering gloom, smoke rises.
I watch as the evidence departs this world.
A funeral of sorts. Saying goodbye to mundane memories,
Once my life of long ago, slipping away in shadows.

More sticks; another bundle of memories ablaze.
My solemn task. Putting the past to bed.
Secrets entrusted to me. Out of respect I dare not look.
The smoke rolls forward and joins the enveloping night.

re/solution

devices

escape

magic

metaphor

peace

perspective/s

re/visions

equilibrium

harmony

collectives

out of the writing room

re/solution

Helen:

We conclude at the beginning! Here are examples of writing in response to the fun, celebratory, energising and inspiring word-games and sound-games that we usually use as starting points or warmups for workshops and groups. However, in a therapeutic context they can serve as an excellent antidote to the examination of 'issues'. This is an important and valuable process, even where it can only serve as temporary distraction from difficulty or pain. Used in other contexts, this kind of approach opens up new expressive possibilities by encouraging experimentation with form, structure, vocabulary and voice. This section therefore contains examples of creative solutions to both creative and personal problems and obstacles. Some of the pieces are also collaborative, partially or wholly dependent upon the group rather than the individual. 'Struggling with a Heavy Load' demonstrates how this can work. Standing in a circle, each member of the group gave a back and shoulder massage to the person in front. Thus relaxed, and with a sensitised 'writing surface', they proceeded to trace the shape of a letter on the back of this person, who then identified it. The recipient then traced another letter, on the back of the person in front of them, until a word was formed, and then another, until it built into a sentence. As we were essentially working with invisible ink, I copied the sentence onto the white-board as it progressed. The only rules were that it should be grammatical — the words themselves did not need to make 'sense' as such; and to stay present with the sensation of giving and receiving the letter on the back, rather than anticipating the finished word. The sentence finally generated by this group read 'they spilled and shoved the wheels of manure at field fitful', which, as one participant pointed out, sounded like something from John Bunyan's 17th century allegory *The Pilgrim's Progress*. Another said, forget the monkeys and the typewriters: this is how *Hamlet* got written! After much hilarity we sat down and everyone wrote a story incorporating as many as possible of the words from the sentence. Given the original words, it wasn't surprising that the theme of agricultural struggle tended to recur, but as Ernie's example shows, 'solutions' can lead back, to new ways of looking at 'challenges'.

Lynn:

Writers find creative ways of dealing with problems in ways I could never have imagined. If you read the first piece in this section you will see what I mean! If people need a little bit of help, I might ask them to literally re-write the past with a different ending; this is what Jan-Sue Robinson does in her pieces about her mother's death. Or I might ask them to abandon the real world and create a magic one where anything is possible. One woman, writing about depression, described her life as a series of paths which always, always led her back to the beginning so I suggested that she conjured up a guardian angel to walk with her and give her support. Writers may not always be able to solve their real-life problems, but in the Writing Room they can experiment with alternative and imaginative answers.

It is important not to leave writers in dark places. If eight or nine sessions have been cathartic and moving, then I will probably make sure that the tenth and last is light-hearted so that everyone leaves the Writing Room with a smile and a wave. Or if a workshop has concentrated for most of the day on the expression of difficult emotion, then at the end we try to achieve a sense of release and resolution. Sometimes I end with mirror movements with writers working in pairs, and finish with a circle dance. Sometimes I play Pass-the-Parcel, or ask writers to bring in a very small gift in a big box. We try to guess what is hidden beneath the string and paper, and tell each other what we would just love to find inside the box. Sometimes there are real gifts – a poppy, an apple-cake and cream, tiny candles. One day we ate smarties.

The Device

Stephanie Taylor

I have many devices or aids for keeping myself on the straight and narrow. I have a special favourite I use if I'm feeling low, frustrated or out of control. It is designed by me, and nobody else has been told about it or used it.

 It is a semi-circle of iron with two claws hinged in at either end. When the device is at rest, the claws point inwards towards each other. They are hinged so that the only way they can move is up.

This is a head-holding device. First you take it by the handle and hold it over your head so one spike goes at the front and one goes directly opposite at the back. Then you push the device down, forcing the claws upwards until you get it into the right position. Then you pull up briskly until the spikes pierce your head and lock into place. Then with one sharp flick movement to the right, you snap off your head and carry it on a relaxed arm down by your thigh where it won't hurt anyone.

The strange thing I've noticed when I am carrying my own head around is that I still look down to see myself holding it.

Hat Power

Olga Mitchell

Wearing my hat
Makes me feel whole
Complete and confident
Able to conduct my life
In a true fashion
The certainty
Allows me to be myself
To hold my head high
No matter what
It comforts me
It is so simple
Just wearing my hat
Protects me
And makes life real

This piece was written after a fun session in which we all brought in hats and scarves, some outrageous and some plain silly. We dressed up so that we became different people, and paraded around the room to show off our new selves. Unlike the rest of us, Olga Mitchell simply put on her own hat and sat composed and smiling.

Voodoo Doll

Fiona Stewart

I am a voodoo doll,
Bound in a wrapping of starched cloth,
Pale, non-colour, dullest of whites,
Rough texture.
Forbidden to touch.

You can't imagine a voodoo doll dancing.

I am stuffed tightly,
Allowing no space for a heartbeat.
My joints restricted,
Rigidly held.
Forbidden to move.

You can't imagine a voodoo doll dancing.

I have dead eyes,
They do not sparkle.
Held in a blank expression,
Ice cold.
Forbidden to connect.

You can't imagine a voodoo doll dancing.

I have a rigid jaw,
It stifles my voice.
My throat is clamped,
Silent life.
Forbidden to speak.

You can't imagine a voodoo doll dancing.

I gain more stuffing,
It stretches the binding,
Exposing my weakness,
Repulsive to others.
Forbidden to attract.

You can't imagine a voodoo doll dancing.

You stick pins in,
They cause sharp pain,
You give me your anger,
I accept.
Forbidden to assert.

You can't imagine a voodoo doll dancing.

You could instead,
Take some time,
Look within the stuffing,
See me soften.
Allowed to hope.

Can you imagine a voodoo doll dancing?

I keep a secret,
A rose quartz,
Hidden deep inside,
Longing to be seen.
Allowed to love.

I can imagine a voodoo doll dancing.

This poem began as an exploration of the differences between inner and outer selves, and ended as a powerful performance piece which we recited to the accompaniment of a drum and a didgeridoo.

Last Night I Slipped into your Dreams

Gabriella Moericke

Last night I slipped into your dreams, unnoticed. Lying next to you, I had felt your heartbeat becoming quicker and quicker, more and more tormented, skipping a beat, frightened.

Slowly I started travelling down on the sounds of your heart, each note carrying me further and further into the depths of your being. Your heart was beating like drums, growing louder and louder while I was approaching a dark dream cloud, until all of a sudden I arrived in the middle of it. I was standing next to you, invisible, seeing the dragon that tormented you. Powerless, paralysed by fear, you were unable to move. I knew instinctively that we could not fight the dragon face on. Swiftly I turned around, running back on the beats of your heart 'til I found myself again in the bed next to you.

Silently, I slipped out of the bed, my feet hardly touching the ground. I managed to glide down the stairs and close the big front door behind me without waking the dogs. And there I stood in the cold dark night, the fresh air clearing my mind. I remembered that I had seen a long ladder in a clearing deep in the forest behind the big trees. Where might it have been? I walked deeper and deeper into the darkness of the woods. Only the moon was guiding me, and the long black shadows of the trees were walking at my side, appearing and disappearing, dancing all around me. Where could I find the ladder? When I came to the clearing I was so tired that I sat down and closed my eyes. Leaning against an old pine tree I could see clearly. There right in front of me I saw the first steps of the white ladder. It rose up into the sky. I could not even see its end. I lifted myself from the ground and, trembling with cold and fear, I slowly pulled myself up, step by step. The higher I got, the lighter I felt, as if I had been given wings. In no time I reached the first stars. And how lucky I was. Right away I found your stars blinking in distress, urgently asking for help. But what was the matter with them? Walking round from star to star, I knew: one star was missing. Had it dropped out of the sky? Had it dissolved into the dark night? Or was it hiding somewhere, cheekily playing around? Do stars play hide and seek? I had no choice. I had to play the game and go searching for it. If only I could find you, little star, then we would be able to fight the dragon and slay it. If only you would shine again, maybe then the dragon would disappear by itself. If you showed yourself then strength and health would flow again through the soul entrusted to you. Silently I waited for a moment, pleading with the missing star to show itself. Nearly giving up, I looked around. A little star appeared from behind me. I was not angry. I was only glad to have found it. I took it gently in my hand and placed it right amongst your stars. I rearranged your stars, adjusting them to catch the light. And as soon as they were reunited they started dancing on the night sky. They danced so joyfully that golden dust fell down to earth.

The next morning when you woke up beside me you had a golden glitter in your eyes. 'Something very special happened to me last night,' you said, beginning your long story of how you had slain your dragon.

In this story, Gabriella, taking her initial inspiration from a beating drum, has created a fantastical tale that eloquently illustrates how effectively disquiet, discomfort, even pain, can find re/solution. The magical setting of the story provides readers with an unexpectedly different perspective from which to view their own experiences of difficult times.

Grief

Stephanie Taylor

I hold my grief in a bucket.

The bucket wobbles in the back of a truck, water slopping around inside, held in by tin and a surface tension threatening to split. The ride is bumpy.

A jolt.

A lurch.

A single droplet leaps over the side. The sloshing body yearns to do the same, bulging and heaving, but like a breath caught before a yawn, it pulls back and settles uneasily into the cold vessel. Straining.

My eyes search desperately for a witness.

Nobody wants it to spill, nobody.

I want to kick it over.

Written in one of a number of classes in which we worked on the translation of emotion into metaphor.

Struggling with a Heavy Load

Ernie

"Piece using the words *wheels, manure, spill, shove, fitful* and *field* randomly generated by the writing group. It unconsciously reflects my desperation as a carer."

The sky was lowering itself down towards the landscape of trees, fields and hedge-rows, and the air tensed. The song of the starlings mingled with the call of the rooks gathering in the copse. In less than half an hour the light would be gone and I could detect wet weather approaching. Desperation caught in my stomach as I pushed at the old wooden cart, mired in the mud and refusing to move, no matter how I pushed and teased it. I tried to lever the wheels forward with a spar from a broken-down fence running along the line of hawthorn. I gave it a shove and leaned on the wood. With a fitful series of jerks and slurps the wheels ran forward before sinking into the mire again. In the gloaming I could see a light go on in the farmhouse kitchen window.

By now my legs were muddied over the tops of my boots and I was sweating. I took a rest, cursing the birds that circled around, throwing down their derision. One final attempt and then I could allow myself to accept defeat. From the lane I picked up a couple of flat stones and placed them under the cart wheels. Using the length of wood I persuaded the wheels to slide onto the stones and I managed to steady the load. As the light faded I moved the cart towards the gap in the hedge but at the last moment it slithered back into a hollow and spilled the load of manure back on to the ground from which I had recently gathered it.

This, like the pieces that follow, demonstrates how creative writing involves both the making of conscious choices, and allowing chance to intervene.

Crackle Mountain

Debbie Hind

Mountain crackle
fountain prattle
hearing cackle
not wanting to tackle
maintain cackle

Crackle mountain
mountains of crackling
burnt pork on a fork
on the plate
crunching in your mouth
the mouth of a river flowing too fast

Mountain crackling
fire flames leaping ever higher
high on a mountain
was it in Mexico?
Angelo?
mountain crackle
acky black ashes

From a brainstorming session where group members called out the words for natural and mechanical sounds and objects, and then experimented with combining and compounding them to coin new phrases.

The Relaxed Toy Tiger

Militza Maitland

The relaxed toy tiger dozed on the shelf. Ann Marie studied it carefully. Was it really relaxed and sleeping? Or just pretending? Tigers are wily creatures – not necessarily to be trusted. Her Aunt Marie, after whom she was named, had given it to her after she had enjoyed Tigger so much in the Winnie the Pooh stories. But Ann Marie was distrustful. Better lock it up in the chest. It was after all a wild creature at heart. It was definitely pretending, she decided as she placed it in the chest and clamped it firmly shut. She gave the chest a little kick for good measure once the tiger was safely inside. She had never liked the creature, and wasn't especially fond of Aunt Marie either, come to that.

And Aunt Marie was calling her now.

'Tea!'

'Coming!'

Now what? What else would she have to be grateful for?

'Have you washed your hands?'

'Yes,' she lied. (How would Aunt Marie know?)

'I've got a surprise for you. Would you like to see it?'

'Oh yes,' Ann Marie replied dutifully, her attempt at pleasure not quite reaching her voice, which fell rather flatly.

She looked around. The table was laid with biscuits and cheese, some watered-down fruit juice, some jam sandwiches. Evidently this was not the surprise. What else could she see? Oh no! She knew what bulky, oddly wrapped parcels meant. Aunt Marie rather prided herself on her way with little knick-knacks and odds and ends that she found in charity shops and bazaars. Her resourcefulness in putting together the most unlikely objects made her the terror of the organisers of the church fete, the annual Christmas bazaar and many other events.

Ann opened it gingerly. It was a boat. The name of the boat was the Ann Marie. It had a stained glass window, a black stone and a rope.

The group generated opening and closing sentences collectively, via a gradual, incremental process too lengthy to describe here and which must therefore remain secret! Then each member wrote their own story to 'join the dots'.

Book of the Dead

C Scott

"Members of the group were asked to walk round the room and note the things that came to their attention in three lists: things liked, things disliked, and things to which they were indifferent. We were then asked to write about one of the objects, as though we liked, disliked, or were indifferent to it; and finally, to present the object in the first person."

(i)

The Book of the Dead: what a marvellous title. See how large it is. But can it really ever be large enough? There are so many dead. Is it on the highest shelf to be nearest Heaven? What images it conjures up of personalities from ages past! Do you think they come here by night to reunite and talk of life? Wouldn't you love to come here by moonlight, light a candle, bring the book down from its high shelf and settle comfortably on a very large cushion to read until the break of day? It would tell us so much.

(ii)

The Book of the Dead. Horrid object. Its black cover indicates that it is full of foreboding. In life, one must never think of death. Death is the end and any book with that title should be banished. Straight into the furnace with it. Burn it. It is an abomination against life and the living.

(iii)

The Book of the Dead. Well, there it is up on its high shelf. I shall pass it by.

(iv)

I am the Book of the Dead. I have a wonderful name. I am the ultimate book. I am so old that I cannot remember how or where I came into being. Somewhere in my mind is an idea that several people were involved in my creation but they are long gone. I was bought centuries ago by someone interested in philosophy and passed down through their family until its line ended. Then someone found me and brought me to 28 Great King Street. Because of my size they put me on the highest shelf where I would not interfere with lesser books. Now I lie here in dignified state watching the procession of life below. From time to time someone notices me on my high shelf and wonders about me. Someone did so this evening. She did not know that I was watching her too and that I have the ability to read human thought. Will she really arrive by moonlight, light her candle and reach up to the highest shelf?

C Scott eloquently describes how this exercise was set up. It is useful as a therapeutic writing tool in times of stress and tension because it encourages the writer to consider things and situations from different points of view, and to see them all as valid.

Jim

Claudine Meyer

Jim's physical characteristics:
Jim has bad skin, pale, lots of minute holes and scars of spots from his teenage years. He has deep wrinkles. All these are the signs of a lifelong poor diet of bacon butties and chips, pints of beer at weekends and lack of outdoor exercise. He used to smoke 40 a day but stopped last year under family pressure. His lips are dry and cracked. Moisturising lotions and gel for chapped lips have never entered his male world.

Jim described in a sympathetic manner:
Jim has a very gentle face. His dark eyes look at you as if a piece of blue velvet had gently brushed your face. And he always looks so neat: clean, well ironed shirts, discreet ties and suits that always seem to be just out of the dry cleaners. His voice is controlled, even: loud enough so that you understand him clearly; firm enough so that you accept his authority willingly. In the winter he wears an anorak; he favours blue. In the summer he wears pastel shirts and brighter ties.

Jim described in an unsympathetic manner:
Jim always looks so neat: impeccable suits, well ironed shirts with neat collars. He has little imagination when it comes to ties. They are often dark blue with discreet little spots or squares in blue or red. His skin is blotchy, pale and greasy, showing a lifelong poor diet of chip butties and hangovers. His hair is mousy, cut into a short back and sides. He always looks stressed. In fact the worry wrinkles are so deep they don't disappear when he smiles. He does not really smile, the right side of his mouth twists upwards and his eyes remain cold, sharp and piercing. He is the kind of person who makes you feel uneasy when he sets eyes on you.

Jim described objectively:
Jim goes home every night at 5.30; not 5.27 or 5.33, 5.30. He drives a

Volvo estate. He goes home the same way, every night, and he has done so for 22 years. He does not even want to go home any more, to boring TV, the same food, the same woman. When was the last time they had sex? Oh yes, a few week-ends ago, just mechanical and no more. He sees the grand-children every Sunday afternoon. He used to go to the pub after work with Dave from HR but he stopped last year. What was the point?

He gets home, goes upstairs, hangs up his suit and tie in the wardrobe, puts his shirt into the dirty washing basket on the landing and puts on his navy blue track suit. Then he goes downstairs into the kitchen, gives Janet a kiss on the right cheek and asks, 'what kind of a day have you had, dear?' He sits down for his tea: haddock, chips, tinned peas and brown sauce, two pieces of white bread, butter and strawberry jam, tinned fruit and a cup of Tetley tea, milk, two sugars. Yesterday it was steak pie.

This and the next piece were written in separate classes, with different facilitators, yet share some similarities. 'Jim' began as another way of looking at something from alternative perspectives. In this case the stimulus was a picture in a newspaper. It demonstrates a way of creating fictional characters unlike oneself and situations outwith one's own experience, as well as how the reader's response is — often unconsciously — affected by the stance of the narrator. 'Buttons' was written during a number of sessions devoted to the development of character. Writers were asked to try this approach as a way of getting to know their characters very well.

Buttons

Fiona Stewart

Sophie, by Jane Elliot, her employer:

Sophie is the best employee I have ever had. She is always on time and will work through her breaks if we are particularly busy. Her manner is gentle which is just perfect, especially for dealing with our older customers. Her dress-sense is really quirky. I like it. I bet she would be good at designing her own clothes given a little bit more confidence. She could always decorate them with buttons – that seems to be her passion.

I am very worried about her not turning up this morning, especially as she hasn't phoned. This is so unlike her.

Sophie, by Mrs Graham, a client at the dressmakers where she works:

She's a very polite girl, kind of non-descript. A bit different from most of the young ones these days. Quiet and reserved, I would say. She certainly does her job well. Once she's measured me for an outfit it never needs re-adjusting. Not like the girl who was here before her. Sometimes I have asked her about her family or social life but she never gives much away. So I can't tell you anything about her background. Definitely not from around here, judging by her accent.

Oh, she does seem to have a thing about buttons, if that's any help.

Sophie, by Mary, her flatmate:

Sophie, she's my flatmate, yeah. Well, I was out late last night so I crashed out this morning. Couldn't tell you whether she left for work or not. To be honest, I don't like her that much. She never comes out for a drink or joins in when I have mates round here. She's tidy and pays the rent on time but I just find her a bit on the boring side. I mean, she collects buttons, for heaven's sake!

Entry in Sophie's diary, 9th February:

I had a strange thought this afternoon. On the way home from work I popped into my favourite charity shop to see if they had any buttons kept aside for me. They had gathered quite a handful but just charged me a pound. Handy since I am running on thin air until pay day. When I got home I decided to tidy out my button collection. It was actually an excuse to stay in my room as Mary was in the flat, music blaring. She must think I am mad but I figure as long as I don't cause her any problems she'll let me stay. Hopefully she'll get bored of trying to persuade me to go out to the pub fairly soon. So, back to my strange thought. I have a section in the button tray for all the ones that don't fit anywhere else, the odd ones. 'That's me,' I thought, 'that's where I belong.' Maybe I should try to find other misfits – they might accept me as one of them – you never know!

My Mother's Death

Jan-Sue Robinson

One

It was the morning of New Year's Eve. The New Year's Eve of all New Year's Eves. The Millennium.

Dave arrived last night. It was wonderful to sleep in his arms. I needed the protection. I had seen and felt more than my share these past few months. I hadn't felt alone with my sisters at my side, but I had felt lonely at times with Dave far away. Dave surprised me with croissants from my favourite Edinburgh patisserie. So thoughtful. We ate in bed and spoke of our months apart; the things you can't express over the phone.

We were jolted back to reality by the phone ringing. Linda's voice was full of despair. 'The doctor has said the end is near. They are predicting between a few hours and a week.' Even though the news wasn't surprising, it was shocking. Up until this moment, the doctors had expressed hope. I asked Linda, 'should we come right away?' 'We need to pace ourselves. It might be a long week. Betty's coming in the next hour. So we've got it covered.'

I desperately needed more private time with Dave so I chose to take Linda at her word and stay a little longer. A peaceful couple of hours passed. Eventually we got dressed and left for the hospital. We drove to the local store first to stock up on provisions. My mobile rang. I answered with trepidation. 'It's over,' Linda said with emptiness in her voice. 'She's dead.'

I dropped the food I was choosing and left Dave behind. Like a robot I ran out of the door into the parking lot. I was stunned, but asked, 'what happened?'

'Betty and I were at her bedside. We watched the rhythm of her breathing as it grew shallower. I noticed how her skin was golden.'

Betty remarked, 'mom looks beautiful.'

Roberta muttered, 'that's because the angels have come to take her.'

'And that was it. A few minutes later mom dies peacefully. That was a few minutes ago. 2.29 pm.'

'I'm only five minutes away. We'll be there soon.'

Dave was behind me looking at me supportively. Of course he knew what had happened without hearing a thing. We drove up and parked for the last time. Walked the corridors decorated for the big event, irrelevant to us.

I opened her door and walked into bustle. Linda, Betty, Roberta, a nurse and the hospital chaplain all milling about, doing nothing. I couldn't take it all in. I had withdrawn to nowhere deep within. After a lengthy minute, Linda said, 'look at her!' She had taken mom's hand and was stroking it as though it were a kitten. It was excruciating to look at her. This wasn't my mom anymore. I did touch her hand. She already felt like a mannequin.

And that's when I lost it. Tears came from deep within, and that set Dave off, and Betty, and quite frankly I can't remember much after that. Busyness. Words, lots of words, but I didn't comprehend any of them.

I was completely empty. A shell. Just like my mother.

Two

It was the morning of New Year's Eve. The New Year's Eve of all New Year's Eves. The Millennium.

Dave arrived last night. It was wonderful to sleep in his arms. I needed the protection. I had seen and felt more than my share these past few months. I hadn't felt alone with my sisters at my side. But I had felt lonely at times with Dave far away. Dave surprised me with croissants from my favourite Edinburgh patisserie. So thoughtful. We ate in bed and spoke of our months apart; the things you can't express over the phone.

We were jolted back to reality by the phone ringing. Linda spoke with deep sincerity in her voice. 'Mom's asking for you.' I responded, 'we'll be there as soon as possible.' I dressed without speaking, staying focused on what I was doing, getting to the hospital in lightning speed. We drove in silence. What can one say at a time like this? We arrived and parked in the valet parking to save time. Walked the corridors decorated for the big event, irrelevant to us.

We opened her door. Linda, Betty and Roberta were there. They smiled with tenderness and sadness in their eyes. We all knew time was passing too quickly. I then looked at mom. She smiled her sweet smile. But she looked different from the day before. She looked at peace. Without thinking, I knew why. I returned my gaze to the others and asked quietly, 'can I have a few minutes alone with mom?' They responded by exiting, one by one.

When we were alone, mom asked me to lie on her bed. She had done this throughout the last few months when she needed a little extra comfort or intimacy. I obliged and perched on the edge so as not to disturb her IV or monitors. I took her hand, so tiny, her nails long and chipped from recent neglect, something she would have hated if she had been able to. We did not look at each other, but sat in silence. It is a special experience when you know you are an emotional oasis for someone you love. My heart was entirely open as I listened to my mother's words.

'You know that I have lived a wonderful life. I have no regrets. I have felt blessed, having the love of my family. That is everything to me. But I am tired. I can't fight any longer. Know that I have loved you more than words can ever say. Do not be sad as there is nothing to be sad about.'

I sat up, turned and looked into her eyes as I spoke.

'Mom, I love you very much. Maybe too much. Maybe you have been holding on so as not to disappoint me. You don't need to anymore. I will miss you more than you will know, but I will never feel alone.'

I bent towards her and saw the tears in her eyes. I kissed her and we smiled. I looked for the last time into the eyes of the woman who bore me and supported me my whole life. I held her hand more fiercely and she responded with one last flurry of love before she shut her eyes.

A few minutes later I got up and opened the door, ushering my family back in. We all stood at her bedside and watched the rhythm of her breathing as it grew shallower. Betty said, 'mom looks beautiful'. Roberta muttered, 'that's the angels coming to take her.'

A few minutes later mom died peacefully. At 2.29 pm, December 31st, 1999.

May she rest in peace.

.

Jan-Sue Robinson was grieving after the death of her mother when she came to the Salisbury Centre group. Lynn suggested that she re-write the actual events so that her pain and frustration were replaced with closure and resolution, allowing her to say goodbye to her mother in the way that she had wanted.

Ashes

Jan-Sue Robinson

The sun sets with vibrancy over the inlet. Deep reds and ochres fill the sky.

We watch, in our own worlds, as we wait for all to arrive. We then walk slowly and silently towards the ocean shoreline. This beach is a major place in my life. Good memories fill my heart. Each time that I return to Florida, I spend time at this beach. It's not that it's spectacularly beautiful, it's that it's a part of me.

I walk ahead of the others. I need to carve a little privacy for myself.

The path becomes a footbridge over scrub-bush and rocks. The footbridge ends with pristine white sand stretching for miles both left and right. Heavy, stagnant clouds fill the sky. The water is dark grey since the sun set.

I have left everyone behind. I walk out into the waves. The water is cold, powerful but bearable, although I am somewhat oblivious anyway. I begin to reflect on the last time I was here. I was with my mother. We sat on the water's edge and spoke and read books and did absolutely nothing. At one point we laughed till we cried – the way I loved to see my mother.

Today is different. I reach into the bag and grab a handful of my mother's ashes. Time stands still. I am submerged in nature and its power, and I begin to cry. So different from my last visit here. Moments pass and I realise the waves are overwhelming me. I turn and walk towards the others who have caught up.

We make a circle, hold hands and say one word that best describes Rena. Kind, gentle, warm, lovely... My sisters scatter the rest of mom's ashes. We hug in silence.

We begin to walk back to the inlet. We have chosen to eat at JB's Fish Camp Restaurant, mom's favourite. The evening ends with warmth, nourishment and laughter. Just as mom told me she would like...when this day came.

Groove

Fiona Stewart

Again I lie in this groove in the dirt,
My own hollow moulded out over time.
In this endless plain of wilderness
Here they come again.

The herd of buffalo rampage over me.
I am beyond fear now, this is so familiar.
Their hooves batter my body to a pulp;
Grit seeps into every pore.

I linger long after the echoes of thundering beasts,
My stillness held beneath a cloud of dust,
Slowly I reform, as always weaker than before.
My breath returns.

At last sunset gives relief
From the baking heat of the desert.
With darkness the crow is back again.
Waiting to pick at my sinewy remains.

Lacking the strength to push him away,
I dare to look into his eyes.
A ray of light from the moon is reflected in them.
It holds me paralysed.

The cold moonlight reaches my skin
Through torn clothes,
Piercing into my heart.
It gives me enough strength to struggle up from the barren earth.

Dazed and bemused I stand upright.
Finding my balance I feel the wind about me.
Leaving the groove behind,
My journey begins.

Autumn in the Meadows

Southside Group

The Southside group set up an alfresco Writing Room on the Meadows on two beautiful Autumn mornings. The aim was to interact with the environment and each other, and to produce writing that worked with the stereotypical blue sky, sunlight on turning leaves, melting frost, etc., and pushed beyond cliché into an authentic, original, personal and collective representation of the occasion.

We divided into two groups. One sat on a bench and observed — and overheard — the passing human traffic, and recorded their data as a stream of consciousness monologue. Some weeks later, when the weather had deteriorated and driven us back to the shelter of the Writing Room we used this material in another session: everyone took a word, line or idea from it as the starting point for their own work. Everyone else strode out onto the middle of one of the lawns and took it in turns to rotate slowly around 360 degrees, calling out the names of everything they noticed whilst another member of the group acted as scribe. The scribe then read out the list and the others called out the first thing they associated with each item on it. Out of this material, still standing on damp grass, they each created a stanza of the collective poem 'Under the Branches.' We re-grouped at the bench and read to each other.

Next, everyone wandered off, with the instruction to turn down their visual alertness and increase attention to the rhythms of their footfall, breath and heartbeat, and to any extraneous sounds and noises, until they arrived at a place to write. After twenty minutes they returned to the bench with widely differing responses. After reading we still had a few minutes left, so we quickly created a spontaneous group piece. One member selected a line or phrase from her own work; another followed with the line from her piece that seemed to make the best link, and so on until we had collaged the collective poem 'The Trees Filter the Sunlight.'

This formed a great basis for the following week's work, which involved spending the whole session creating a more formal group structure (very) loosely based on the Japanese form of Renga. We generated the first stanza by standing still on the path in the Meadows, as the poem says, each creating a line that seemed to give the essence of the present moment. Then we dispersed, each to write material for the first 'link', two lines that followed on from the opening. Re-grouping at our bench, we considered everyone's offering and selected that which we felt formed the most suitable link. Then off we went again to write, and then choose, the next link, and so on. Alternating between two- and three-line stanzas, and between the roles of writer and editor, we encapsulated the human and natural world, the formalities and irregularities, that constituted the Meadows for us on that particular morning.

Back at the Southside Centre next week, the Writing Room became the Editing Suite. We divided into two groups — which included some members who had not attended the Meadows sessions — to play with and work on 'Under the Branches' and 'The Trees Filter.' The original intention was for both groups to spend about twenty minutes on each piece, discussing the parts and the whole, the wood and the trees: attending to details of grammar, punctuation and diction, whilst remaining alert to overall sense. Then we would collate our findings and agree on a final version of each poem. It quickly became clear that this was not going to happen, as participants discovered how substituting a word or altering a tense can have wider ramifications for the whole piece. In the end — after quite a few disagreements over the details — we agreed that it wasn't possible to arrive at one version of each poem because the two groups had come up with quite different solutions. So here are the original, and two edited versions of each Meadows poem, followed by the Renga.

i. Under the Branches

Under the branches of the tall trees
I gazed along the maze
With its innumerable confusing footpaths.

I saw soggy shadows, warm food in a red shop and boys and girls with healing
scabs.

Winding winds blow through the turret
Round lamp-posts
To Debbie sitting on the bench.

Version One

Above the branches of the tall trees
I gazed along the maze
And its many confusing footpaths;

Saw soggy shadows, smelt warm food served from a red shop, heard tots with
weeping scabs.

Winds blew round lamp-posts
Through the turret
To mothers sitting on the bench.

Version Two

Above the branches of the tall trees
I gaze along the maze
With its infinite confusing paths.

Soggy shadows, warm bread from the corner shop, boys and girls with healing
scabs.

Winds swirl through turrets
Embracing invisible companions
Sitting with Debbie on the bench.

ii. The Trees Filter

The trees filter the sunlight into a shadow mosaic on the grass
A bubble of silent tranquillity, tolerant but not integrating
Brisk footsteps of the young and the faltering footsteps of the old
Hopscotch ping-pongs back and forth
When I will no longer hear the sound of someone softly hitting a tennis
ball.

Version One
When will I no longer hear the sound of someone softly hitting a tennis
ball;
See trees filter sunlight into a mosaic on clipped grass?
Stuck in my bubble of disintegrating tranquillity
Hoscotch pingpongs now and then.
My faltering footsteps hear brisk footsteps of the young.
When will I no longer hear the sound?

Version Two
The trees splinter harsh sunlight into a mosaic shadow.
A space on a bench between sound and silence.
Brisk footsteps of the young and the faltering footsteps of the old,
When I will no longer hear the sound of someone softly hitting a tennis
ball,
Or children hop-scotching back and forth.

iii. Meadows Renga

Standing still on the path in the Meadows
As an old man hurries past
The sun warms our backs, casting lengthy shadows.

A scattering of gold, green, yellow leaves has fallen
From a regimented line of solid trees.

Avenues of lamp-posts stagger
Trying to keep order over geometric lawns
But a woman drops litter by the bin.

Plastic bags somersault over damp grass
Ignored by a woman catwalking the path.

A woman pushing a buggy looks up briefly
As two businessmen jog across her path.
Then she glances away as she lets them pass.

Footballboot studs pock the grass.
I raise my eyes to birdsong and see no clouds.

Nurture

Salisbury Centre Group

Dancing in the rain
Dancing through pain
Laughing
Feet touch soil
And walk between flowers

I float backwards
In time
And still
Move forwards
Both old and young

I can guide
Another
To a new land
With the touch of my hand
Looking into different eyes
I see myself
Mirrored

Under the sun
I nurture myself
Like the wind blowing
Like the cradle rocking
Like a mother caring
Like a rose opening

Like the birth of a butterfly.

The Middle-Aged Man and the Sea: A Fable

Chris Korycinski

Once upon a time, when the sun shone just as it does now, but more fiercely, and the wind blew just as it does now, but more strongly, and when people spoke with the trees and oceans, there lived a man whose parents – in a moment of madness or of divine inspiration – named him Philadelphus. Burdened with this name he grew up being teased and laughed at by all (just as you would be teased and laughed at if you had been given this name).

He grew to despise the people who had treated him so badly and disliked his parents who had given him this name; yet, because of his work as an inn-keeper, he had to hide his feelings from most people (just as you have to hide your feelings from others at times, too). But he had one friend in his life who always treated him kindly and with respect, who spoke comforting words when Philadelphus couldn't bottle up his feelings any more and felt compelled to pour out his troubles. This friend was the sea.

Every morning at dawn, before he started work, and every dark evening when work for the day was done, he went to talk with the sea and ask her to take him away so that he could find happiness. And after he had spoken and made his plea the sea would brighten as if a cloud had cleared from in front of the sun, and the waves would grow higher and higher, their crests finally revealing the silver and opal-studded tips of the crown of the Queen of the Sea. And she would reply in words neither deep nor shallow, neither wide nor narrow, neither distant nor close, neither inside nor outside, but in the manner and with words that only the Queen of the Sea could speak, and she would say, 'this time I shall not, this time I will not, but this time cannot last. And then you will come to me and I to you'. Philadelphus was always both saddened and uplifted by this answer; saddened that the time had not yet come, but uplifted by the knowledge that promises for the future would be fulfilled.

One day, which seemed to be no different from any other day, Philadelphus went to the sea at dawn and asked her to take him away, just as he had done for so many years. Yet on this day the sea did not brighten, the waves rose no higher and the silver and opal tips of the crown of the Queen of the

Sea did not appear. The waves continued to talk to each other with their muttering, murmuring voices, just as they had always talked amongst themselves, but even they would not vouchsafe him a reply. Looking again out to the empty horizon, he asked the sea once more, and as before, silence was his only reward. Saddened and disappointed, he turned his face away from the sea and back to the land where his day's work lay, making his way to the inn once again. For the rest of the week he went to the sea every morning and every evening, just as he had always done, yet each day no voice spoke to him; the Queen of the Sea did not appear.

He was distraught: how could he continue without the hope of release? Each day when he went to the sea he thought to himself that this day would be the one when the Queen of the Sea would answer and each day his disappointment and misery increased as no answer came. People in the town who had laughed not only at his name but also at his foolish pleas to the sea, now became concerned as he grew thinner and thinner, sadder and sadder and more and more withdrawn. Soon they stopped coming to his inn – they wanted enjoyment, not sadness; cheerfulness, not gloom. Philadelphus didn't care. 'Without hope for the future what is the point of the present?' he thought to himself as he looked at the dark, empty, cheerless tavern. Yet he knew that one possibility remained, a possibility which he had previously dismissed but which became more and more real as his despair increased; he would look for the Queen of the Sea and ask why she had abandoned him. Had he done something wrong? Had she changed her mind about taking him away? He felt he needed to know the answers even if they saddened him and were not the ones he wanted to hear. He needed to know the answers even if he risked his life searching for them.

He looked about the empty and unwelcoming inn – here was plenty of drink, there was plenty of bread, meat, of pickled and preserved food. These could be provisions for a small boat – he could survive on them. He could go out on the sea and search for the Queen and demand an answer to his question.

The people who knew him were amazed. Some thought him mad, others thought him foolish, but everyone was convinced that he could only be going to his death. 'Philadelphus,' they said, 'you have no experience of the sea; you will come to grief. You will lose your way; your boat will sink; you will run out of food; you will die of thirst.' But Philadelphus was determined to have his way and provisioned his boat with food and drink from the inn until it rode heavy and low in the water. 'There,' he thought, 'I will not go hungry or thirsty even if it takes me a long, long time to find the Queen of the Sea.' Yet even now, when it was clear that he would soon be sailing, people in the town asked him to reconsider; and if truth be told he, too, was starting to have doubts about the journey and was astonished, and secretly pleased, by the number of people who seemed to care about him. But having made his decision, he was determined to stick to it (just as you and I, out of pride, sometimes stick to a decision even when it is starting to look a little foolish).

At last the time came for him to depart. He returned to the inn one more time, looked around the empty rooms, the bare shelves, and realised how happy he would be to leave and how much he would miss living here; how people had teased him for so many years, yet how they might not have meant it as cruelly as he thought they did. One last look: 'nothing left, so go.' With that thought he crossed the room one last time, opened the door to the street one last time, stepped though the doorway one last time, but locked the door from the outside for the very first time. And leaving the key with William the Boatbuilder, who worked close by, he walked along the straight cobbled street until he came to the small harbour where his boat lay moored.

The people of the town were already gathered around. 'Philadelphus,' one said, 'let me help you take the provisions back to the inn.' 'No, let me help you,' said another. Then there was a chorus of voices suggesting this, suggesting that, suggesting that he should stay, suggesting that he was a fool, suggesting that they could join him. The words buzzed around Philadelphus' head, filling the air and making it difficult for him to breathe; he knew he had to go, to leave all this behind and seek ful-fillment of the hopes given to him by the Queen of the Sea. So looking neither right nor left, he stepped into his boat, loosened the sail, untied the ropes fore and aft which held it to the harbour, to the town, to his past. He let the boat drift slowly away from land, its sail waving to the people on shore as it caught the wind, then steadying its motion and surging into the future.

Many days passed and with each day, Philadelphus grew more and more confident in piloting the boat. When the wind dropped he knew to add more sails; when it blew more strongly he was swift in taking them down to prevent the mast from snapping or the boat from capsizing. Yet the longer he was on the sea the more disturbed he became at the emptiness around him. The waves continued their never-ending chatter, but did not deign to include him in their conversations; the wind blew, but its indifferent passing was merely part of its travels to distant shores to attend to other matters. If truth be told, Philadelphus was lonely – more lonely than he had been in the town, more lonely than he had ever been in his life.

With greater and greater urgency, every morning and every night he called out to the Queen of the Sea, asking her to reply, but no reply came. And as each morning and each evening passed he found himself growing not only more and more lonely but more and more anxious, more and more worried. He was beset by doubts (the way you can have doubts when things don't go the way you thought they would).

Then one morning on a day which seemed to be just like any other day, but was somehow different, he rose and called out to the Queen of the Sea. As he looked ahead to the east, he saw that on this day, in the closely far distance, there seemed to be a mist – a mist which appeared to grow thicker and more dense in one place, only to become thinner elsewhere; first concealing, then revealing. He looked behind him to the west and it was just the same. To the north? Yes, it was there too. And the south? Of course. He sat there, freed of doubts and happy at last, knowing that all his efforts had borne fruit, for all around were islands – islands whose true name no-one knew (and many thought to be sailors' fables), though all called them the Islands of Hope.

It no longer mattered which way he steered the boat, for he was ringed by the bright horizon of hope and his destination surrounded him; once he reached the islands he would find the answer he looked for. Relaxing for the first time in his long journey, he let the boat move of its own accord towards his goal.

Hours, then days, passed, but his goal came no nearer, nor did it move further away. But this had ceased to worry him for he knew that all he needed was patience and time. Then he would be able to find an answer to his question, he would be able to ask the Queen of the Sea. But one night, a night which was like the other nights he had spent in his boat, but darker, the wind blew as it had done during his voyage, but more fiercely, and the waves grew higher, as they did when the Queen of the Sea was about to appear, but more forbiddingly, and the little boat started to be tossed from wave to wave, like a plaything of the gods. Philadelphus was frightened. He called out to the Queen of the Sea, but the wind shredded his words; he called out to the wind, but it was unconcerned and untroubled by his fears; he called out to the waves, but even if they heard him, their anger was not assuaged. Water started to enter the boat; the planks of the hull started to loosen.

Philadelphus lay on the border of the sandy shore and the rich forest. He realised that he had lost everything; his boat with all its provisions had gone and he himself had been so battered by the storm that there was little life left in him – he knew that he would die soon. He thought wryly of the name of the islands – the Islands of Hope should have been called the Islands of Despair. There was nothing left for him; he realised that he had given everything up for some foolishness and now even his life would be forfeit. All his dreams of meeting the Queen of the Sea? Nothing but imagination. His journey? The journey of a fool. He gazed at the ocean once again. It was now calm, showing no evidence of its recent fury, but as he looked it seemed to lighten, as if a cloud had cleared from in front of the sun, and the waves grew higher and higher, their crests finally revealing the silver and opal-studded tips of the crown of the Queen of the Sea. And she spoke to him in words neither deep nor shallow, neither wide nor narrow, neither distant nor close, neither inside nor outside, but in the manner and with words that only the Queen of the Sea could speak, and she said, 'this time I shall, this time I will, and this time has come. Will you give up all you have and come with me?'

Closing his eyes, Philadelphus smiled to himself; what was there to give up? Everything was gone; nothing was left. He lay back, tired. His mind was empty, and maybe because of this, or maybe for no reason whatsoever except that the right time had come, he felt for the first time the strain he always carried in his hands. He felt how they were curled up as if always grasping, always holding on to something, not letting go, not relinquishing. Slowly un-curling the fingers of his left hand, Philadelphus released his hopes – hopes of the future yet to be, hopes for the now of the present, the ghosts of hopes of the past. He felt them taken on the cool breeze, taken away from him and turned into nothing but air. Now his right hand opened, and promises tumbled over each other, escaping confinement and flying into freedom: promises made, promises broken, promises yet to be fulfilled, promises of his own, promises of others to which he had clung — all disappeared into the cold breeze.

Through his closed eyelids he saw the ocean become lighter still, lighter than he had ever known it. The waves drew back from the shore, 'aaahh…', then surged forward, 'yessss…'.

The wind turned icy.

It was William the Boatbuilder, on one of his usual walks along the seashore, who found Philadelphus' body lying on the bare shingle beach, scarcely more than two miles from the town, from the harbour, from his inn. People came, gathered his body and carried it back. Some talked amongst themselves and nodded in agreement that such foolishness could only have come to an unpleasant end. Some used Philadelphus as a threat to their children: 'If you don't behave then Philadelphus will come in his boat and take you away with him.' Some were sad; many didn't care. A few – maybe those who too wanted to escape the town and its people – thought that it was better that he had died in pursuit of his dream than to have remained safely discontented in his inn, and perhaps even felt envious of him.

The burial was a simple one. All the people present had known Philadelphus because in those days, in those times, people living in the same town all knew each other. They knew what he wanted in life (or they thought they did, anyway) and did their best to give him at least a shadow of this in death. So they did not bury him near the inn he had kept, but remote from it, not within view of the town, but within sight of the sea, at which he had looked with such longing all his days. Flowers on the grave formed a simple memorial.

William came back the next day. The grave still had its few flowers, though many were starting to wilt in the morning heat. He took something small and rounded from his pocket and made a hole, not too deep and not too shallow, at the head of the grave. Placing the object in the hole, he covered it with more soil. 'Let this be a memento of Philadelphus,' he thought, 'in time it may grow and not fade like the flowers.'

Time passed, as it does in small towns, with people working at their work, gossiping with their companions, making friends and making enemies, so it wasn't until the next year that William returned to Philadelphus' grave. He was unsure what to expect; he had heard stories, he had heard rumours, he had heard envy, he had heard fear. He had to see for himself and know the truth – after all he would have to take some of the blame (if, indeed, there was any blame to be given or taken). Climbing up the hill, he turned in the direction of the grave. He stopped, staring awestruck at the mature oak which had grown where there was nothing the year before. It had the appearance of a tree a century old, yet he knew that he had planted the acorn himself only last year. He could see why people were nervous, why they regarded the tree with uncertainty. It was straight, it was strong, it was beautiful, it was all that a perfect oak should be; but it was also unnatural, and so was a source of fear.

Should the tree be avoided? Cut up and destroyed? Left as it was? Everyone had their own opinion; all disagreed (the way we all find disagreement prevails whenever there is a choice to make about our actions). It seemed to William that as the fault was his, he should offer a solution. 'What if I used the tree to build a boat?' he suggested. 'I will cut it down and it will be gone, but it will also remain; it will be destroyed, yet it will live in the boat itself.' Who could deny that this was the perfect solution? The townsfolk had to do nothing for themselves: someone else would do all the work for them, would take all the risks for them. The new boat would bring some extra prosperity to the town. There was nothing to lose, so they quickly agreed before William could change his mind.

And so it happened. The tree was cut (though no-one save William was brave enough to do it) and was brought down from the hill, across the town and to the boatyard by the sea, just across from where Philadelphus had kept his inn. William studied the tree, examined the way the grain of wood ran, looked at how best to cut it, decided which parts of the tree would be used to make this or that part of the boat. 'These will be planks for the hull. That will be some of the decking. And this I will make into a figurehead.' And so he set to work, giving some of the simpler jobs to his apprentices and the more difficult work to the journeymen, but saving the carving of the figurehead for himself. With such beautiful timber he knew that this boat could be the envy of all, so he impressed on everyone the need to take care and to be sure that none of the wood was wasted.

With that swift assurance of people who have worked together for many years the men and boys started to transform the wood. The ribs, the hull the deck all took shape – planks were cut and fitted so easily that all the men were astonished at how quickly the work progressed, almost as if the boat wanted itself to be built. William was less lucky, though. The boat was all but finished, but carving the figurehead was proving a real test of his ability. When he moved his chisel forwards, it veered off to the right or to the left; if he carved the wood to the left the chisel would move forwards or to the right; if he carved to the right then the path of the chisel was equally uncertain. He sharpened his tools time and again, yet still they would not cut how he wanted them to, moving almost as if they had a mind of their own.

He had spent a week in this frustrating work, getting more and more angry with himself and with the wood. After all, he was the one who had told the men to be careful and not waste the precious oak, yet here he was, unable to carve a simple figurehead. He stepped down from the all-but-finished boat to sharpen his tools once again when he saw some of the journeymen gawping at the figurehead. Convinced that they were amused at his inept work, he was about to vent his anger and frustration on them when he realised that they were not laughing at him nor at his work. Instead they were staring open- mouthed at the figurehead. William stepped back away from the boat to join the men, turned to look where they were looking and saw what they were seeing. 'It must be a trick of the evening light,' he thought. Then he turned to one of the men and asked, 'Tell me, what do you see?' The man continued to gawp, his mouth open, unable to form any words. 'Fool!' shouted William, who was by now at the end of his tether, 'tell me what you see!' But there was no need for a reply for everyone could see that the figurehead was very far from usual; not a woman, but a man; not a young, attractive figure, but one which was middle-aged and had seen life; not a pretty face but rather one which looked forward into the future with happiness and keen anticipation. A face they all knew, but transformed by joy.

Contributors' profiles:
the writers in their own words

Ajak
Mother of three who lives and works in Edinburgh, Ajak started writing after her art degree dissertation made her determined never to put her pen back down.

Ann Vilen
Ann teaches creative writing in the USA. When she and her husband arrived in Edinburgh for a six month sabbatical, Ann felt uprooted and lost, and questioned how a temporary move could provoke such unsettled feelings and lead to the exploration of identity, confidence and self-esteem.

Barbara Stone
Edinburgh born and bred, Barbara Stone attended classes at the Salisbury Centre for several terms.

Chris Korycinski
I have worked in a variety of jobs ranging from astrologer to computer researcher but never had any thought of wanting to write after the misery of school essays and O-levels. It was almost forty years before I wrote fiction again and 'The Middle-Aged Man and the Sea' is my third story.

Claudine Meyer
Claudine was born in Paris in 1948. She has lived in Scotland since 1970. She has a house in Provence. She is a consultant in Neuro Linguistic Programming, and has a degree in literature, as well as business and teaching qualifications. Her main areas of interest are self awareness, positive thinking and personal development.

C MacLaverty
Born in Belfast, she now lives in Glasgow. She has had ME for half her life. She writes occasional short stories and poetry. She likes good conversation and sunshine.

C Scott

A peripatetic Scot, now living in Edinburgh, who hopes to devote more time to writing before written language deteriorates into abbreviated text and the spoken word into unintelligible grunts.

Debbie Hind

Originally from Yorkshire, and after many different jobs and pursuits, Debbie moved to Scotland 15 years ago. Now living in Edinburgh with her husband and three sons, she loves writing poetry and short stories.

Elke Williams

Elke was born in Germany, and is married with three sons. Her varied career has included social-work and teaching. She is currently working as a complementary therapist. She started writing when she was hospitalised for depression.

Ernie

is 45 and lives in Leith. For a long long time he was a civil servant and cared for his wife. Now he's studying landscape and is looking forward to life.

Felicity Milne

Born in Biggar, Lanarkshire in 1943, now living in Fife, Felicity Milne writes essentially about 'life', her narrative voice taking inspiration from her own experience and as an observer of others. She has written a collection of poetry and also a short story.

Fiona Stewart

Fiona thought that the creativity she had enjoyed writing stories as a child had got lost when she 'grew up'. Now she realises you don't need to be grown up all of the time and is looking forward to a future exploring her childhood wonder.

Gabriella Moericke

works as a counsellor, hypnotherapist and Louise Hay Trainer in Edinburgh. In her work as well as in her creative writing she aims at transforming life's challenges into enriching experiences of deep love and joy. We are transported into the magic layer of Life.

Hazel MacPherson

Born in the Highlands in 1950, her surroundings gave her the inspiration to start writing poetry and short stories. She eventually moved to Edinburgh, where she now lives with her husband and son.

Helga T Thomson

Helga is half-German and half-Irish. Her family and friends are pleased she has the Irish sense of humour and the German sense of efficiency, and not the other way round. She curently lives in Edinburgh with her Scottish husband and Irish black cat.

Jan-Sue Robinson

is an American who has recently come to Edinburgh. She attended the writing group at the Salisbury Centre.

Judith Fox

works in a left-brained environment but she lives her personal life in her right mind. She dreams her ideal life into being down by the sea in Dunbar.

Lisa Mayber

attended the Salisbury Centre group.

Mandy Calder

Lapsed writer who still believes in the power of the written word… I am somewhere along the healing path that is not quite so dark as where I was when I wrote 'Buried'. At last there is a lot of light back in my life! I live in Edinburgh and am now back to working as a nurse. I enjoy walks with my dog, cycling, running and catching up with friends. I'd like to offer hope to anyone reading these pieces who feels life just ain't worth it. It is!!

Marjorie Wilson

At 93 years of age, Marjorie Wilson has long outlived the normal span of years. She is a published writer and editor, and used to work as a potter. As a regular contributor to *Scots Magazine*, she travelled widely around the islands and mainland. She can still scribble a bit, and lives for her cat, Tufty.

Maureen Lockhart

attended the Salisbury Centre group.

Militza Maitland

If I brought the same imagination to my writing as I do in finding imaginative ways of not writing I would be much further down the road by now! I was initially inspired by Crysse Morrison who led a writers' workshop on a Greek island a couple of years back. Perhaps I also need to be in the sun to be inspired.

M R McDonald

has been writing since her early teens and is a teacher with a joint Hons. MA in English Literature and Philosophy. In 1983 she won the Triennial Calder Verse prize at Aberdeen University and has published her poems in various publications including a small book of 40 of her collected poems. Her work was also broadcast some years ago on *McGregor's Gathering* on Radio 4.

Olga Mitchell

Writing for me is a form of expressing my feelings, whether joyful, playful, lonely or sad. It enriches my life, creating balance and harmony, enabling me to be in tune with myself.

Paula Cowie

attended some of the earliest Writing Room classes at the Salisbury Centre. She established Eco-Building in Fife and is concerned with environmental issues.

Stephanie Taylor

Stephanie loves to write and draw and aspires to combine the two successfully. She would love to live in the countryside with her husband and yummy children.

Susan Bowyer

Born in Fife and returned to the coast after some adventures. Works in Natural Health and Therapies. Writing gives her the freedom to let her thoughts become reality.

Tom Britton

is a 35 year old Glaswegian who finds himself living in Leith after living in Glasgow, New York, Iona and Fife. Tom has many interests including football (Thistle and Scotland), cinema, writing/reading, and supporting the Malt Whisky Society. He even occasionally travels into the City of Edinburgh.

The Editors

Helen Boden

Helen was born in Yorkshire in 1964 and has a degree and doctorate in English. She moved to Edinburgh in 1995 to teach and research Scottish Literature, having previously worked in university English and Continuing Education (Lifelong Learning) departments in Newcastle upon Tyne and Bristol. Her specialisms include poetry, autobiography, travel writing and women's writing. She has published on all these topics, and has edited Dorothy Wordsworth's *Continental Journals*. She has also lived in North-West Sutherland, where the experience of life on the margins of Europe influenced both her creative writing and her eventual decision to leave a career in 'mainstream' education. Currently studying for a counselling qualification, she has a longstanding interest in the therapeutic values of creativity. She enjoys music, hillwalking and good food.

Lynn Michell

Lynn was an army child who grew up in Liverpool, Devon, Kenya, Tripoli, Portsmouth, Germany and Cyprus, attending seventeen schools along the way. She has a degree in English Literature, M.Sc in Educational Psychology, and a doctorate in Psychology. In another life she worked as a university lecturer, educational psychologist, and research fellow in medical sociology, usually writing a book at the same time. In 1987 she became ill with ME. A return to academic work seven years later triggered a severe relapse. Nowadays she experiences immense satisfaction and joy facilitating writing classes and workshops. Lynn has published five projects, fiction and non-fiction, including a writing scheme for schools: *Write From the Start* (six pupil books and two teachers' books), *Growing Up in Smoke, Letters To My Semi-Detached Son, A Stranger At My Table,* and *Shattered: Life with ME.* She relaxes by playing with stained glass, gardening, sailing and walking her two wonderful dogs.

Helen and Lynn are available to facilitate writing workshops and undertake commissions.